Eyewitness
to the
Gods

WHAT I KEPT SECRET FOR DECADES

Erich von Däniken

NEW
PAGE

First published 2015 in German by Kopp Verlag

First English Edition Published by Disinformation Books, an imprint of Red Wheel Weiser

This edition first published in 2019 by New Page Books, an imprint of

Red Wheel/Weiser, LLC

With offices at:
65 Parker Street, Suite 7
Newburyport, MA 01950
www.redwheelweiser.com

ISBN: 978-1-63265-168-6

Library of Congress Cataloging-in-Publication Data available upon request.

Cover design by Howard Grossman
Interior by Maureen Forys, Happenstance Type-O-Rama
Typeset in Eames Century Modern and Praktika

Printed in the United States of America
LB

10   9   8   7   6   5   4   3   2   1

CONTENTS

ILLUSTRATIONS

LETTER TO
MY READERS

Dear Reader,

What actually inspired me to write a controversial book like *Erinnerungen an die Zukunft* (*Memories of the Future*, published in the US as *Chariots of the Gods*)? Who helped me? How do I know that Jesus, the founder of the Christian religion, did not ascend to heaven? Who taught me that the much-praised original texts do not exist at all? How did I come to have pictures of Jesus's tomb? Is it true that the former director of the Egyptian antiquities administration, Dr. Holeil Ghaly, personally led me into the secret chamber of Pharaoh Sekhemkhet, member of the third dynasty? That as a nineteen-year-old, I experienced something uncanny in the country on the Nile? That the story of the robot Upuaut, who discovered a shaft in the pyramid on March 22, 1993, was already known to me before that date? That Rudolf Gantenbrink, who developed the robot, and I are old friends? Did the highly official antiquities administration, along with the DAI (*Deutsches Archäoligisches*

Institut)—the German Archaeological Institute—blatantly lie to me?

Is it correct that I wanted to carry out a helicopter expedition on the upper Amazon and was lied to and deceived? That in Brazil, several acquaintances of mine were murdered? Is it true that a Catholic priest states that he has seen tombs of aliens? Why was it me who found out about the so-called Band of Holes in the Pisco Valley of Peru? How did I bribe a Colombian air force general? And why did the old Salesian priest Carlo Crespi in Cuenca, Ecuador, trust me?

Did I actually speak at many universities? How did the Ancient Astronaut Society (AAS) come into existence? In Germany and in the US, there were highly toxic pamphlets put out against my book—what has become of them? Who authored them? What were the reasons behind doing so? In 1984, was I actually in the secret American base of the then so-called Space Command? What was going on there? Did I really know NASA's rocket builders personally? From the father of space travel, Dr. Hermann Oberth, to Wernher von Braun? Which scientists, astronauts, and cosmonauts support me?

Why in the world do politicians and judges shamelessly violate their respective constitutions? Do we live in an environment of bought journalists? And what about the eternal UFO stories? Have they not long ago been scientifically refuted? Does not everyone know that UFO believers can only be nutcases?

That's how I begin: people are treated like first-class idiots. From the anti-UFO lobby as well.

Cordially!

Erich von Däniken

CHAPTER 1

Impossible Encounters

In which you will learn about the following:

*A Haunting at 36,000 Feet • Pseudo-Science
Without End • Time Machine? • A Baffled
Sheriff • The Never-Ending Case of B and
B Hill • A Visit from Zeta Reticuli •
A Desperate Nick Pope • Professor with Civic
Courage: A Visit from the Father of Space Travel
• A Movie from the Cockpit*

A HAUNTING AT 36,000 FEET

November 7, 1986. The Boeing 747, Japan Airlines flight number 1628, flew at an altitude of 36,000 feet on route to Anchorage, Alaska, local time 5:06 pm. Out of nowhere, just a few miles away from the plane, a bright light suddenly flared up. The Japanese captain, his copilot, and the flight engineer assumed it was a military object. But then, in the distance, they saw colorful lights appear, circling around the bright light. When they checked with ground control, they were told nothing had been detected on radar and that their flight path seemed clear.

But the lights grew larger at a frightening pace. The captain asked the control tower in Anchorage for permission to move to a lower altitude. The plane descended 3200 feet, at which point the strange lights disappeared, as if they had been switched off. The crew on the jumbo jet breathed a sigh of relief and requested to climb back to the original altitude, but just then, two lights raced directly toward their plane.

On the jumbo jet's left side, a brown, billowing light appeared, as if a dim lamp had been turned on. For a moment, the captain thought something was on fire. He pressed his forehead against the cockpit window and couldn't believe his eyes: right next to the plane, moving at the same altitude and speed, was a brownish-orange object. Breathless, the pilot described what was going on to the tower in Anchorage. The tower checked the radar and reported that they could detect an enlarged radar echo. Then, something completely mind-boggling happened—the brown-orange light went out suddenly, as quickly and inexplicably as it had appeared. The three men in the cockpit stared at each other and breathed a sigh of relief. But a moment later, the eerie encounter occurred again, this time on the right side of the plane. At this point, Anchorage radar control also realized that drama was unfolding at 36,000 feet. They reported the incident to the US Air Force and ordered the captain to immediately make the approach to Anchorage . . .

—

During the same timeframe as this incident, from mid-October to mid-December 1986, I was on a lecture tour visiting various US universities. I was accompanied by Geraldine, a lovely young lady who had been assigned to me by Bantam Books, my American publisher. She had, in a very professional manner, cleared many obstacles out of my way. One day, after I finished airing a TV show, Geraldine told me that a Japanese airline captain had called the publisher to try to get in touch with me and had requested that I call him back. Geraldine said it sounded as if it was an important matter and, looking at me inquisitively, asked: "Are you interested?" I nodded, vaguely remembering having read something in a newspaper about an incident involving a Japanese plane.

On December 8, 1986, in an Italian restaurant in Los Angeles, I met with the pilot. He seemed a trustworthy gentleman and was of medium height, with raven-black hair and small wrinkles covering his face. He asked Geraldine, who was with me, to give the two of us privacy. He introduced himself as Kenju Terauchi, and without me asking for ID, he presented his passport and plastic Japan Airlines ID, which identified him. He seemed nervous and kept looking around as if someone was following him.

I found out quickly that he didn't really want to talk to just anyone about the incident. He stated that he and his flight crew had been required to sign forms with the American authorities that swore them to secrecy about the incident under threat of imprisonment for up to ten years and a life-long professional ban if they broke their silence. He had seen me on television, he said approvingly, and had immediately bought each of my books that were available in Japanese. Apart from his family and some close friends, I was the only person he wanted to talk to about the incident. I promised him my absolute discretion until his death (Kenju Terauchi has since passed away).

It was then that he related the details of his frightening experience that he knew scientifically trained people would classify as absolute nonsense. Terauchi first stated that prior to this experience, he had not believed in UFOs at all. He had had no time for silly things like that. His opinion, however, changed drastically after his inexplicable encounter that November evening. He said that the light in front of them had appeared quite unexpectedly and had begun to blind the crew the bigger it grew. He had sat in the cockpit on the left side of the plane, his copilot Takanori Tamefuji had sat on the right, and flight engineer Yoshio Tsukuda had been behind them. When they called in the encounter, none of them could understand why Anchorage radar control could not detect anything on their screens.

He went on to state that a brownish-orange glow had appeared suddenly on his left. From the cockpit window, his view to the rear was very limited; he could not even see the two engines. I asked about the passengers, all of whom must have been eyewitnesses.

"There were no passengers," Terauchi replied. "JAL flight number 1628 was a cargo flight from Paris to Tokyo. We carried French wines and several containers of textiles."

"So you were watching the outer shell of this strange object? How did it look? Metallic? Were there lights or windows?" I pressed on.

"None of that," Terauchi explained. "From the outside, the thing really reminded me of a gigantic walnut. Brown and covered with many furrows. Nothing, really, nothing at all, that hinted at the technology."

I learned that the eerie UFO had been flying for several minutes on his side of the cockpit, at the same speed as the plane, or around 900 kilometers/560 miles per hour. Terauchi and his crew had plenty of time to watch it. One of them even took pictures. They weren't able to estimate the overall size of the object because the UFO's outer skin went out of view behind the wing tips.

"But that thing must have been huge—about the size of an aircraft carrier," he said.

Then the apparition suddenly disappeared, and shortly thereafter, it reemerged on the right side of the plane, just as if the alien power wished that the pilots would have plenty of time to gawk at the spooky object and photograph it as well.

Overall, he said, the terrifying encounter lasted about 30 minutes. It seemed to go on forever. Finally, Terauchi moved the plane along a long trajectory to home in on Anchorage's guiding beam. At 23,000 feet, the crew recognized the distant lights of the city, and suddenly, as if someone had pulled a curtain shut, the lights of the city disappeared. The huge UFO had latched onto the same trajectory as theirs right in front of them; for eight terribly long seconds, it flew in front of them and then veered off over the top right side of the plane.

"The thing was playing cat and mouse with us. We did not see where it finally went; we could no longer observe it," Terauchi explained.

After landing in Anchorage, the crew was taken to a special building outside the airport. They were treated kindly and offered tea, whiskey, and sandwiches.

Kenju Terauchi really wanted to call his superiors in Tokyo, but Anchorage reassured him that they had already been contacted. Time and again, several different gentlemen visited them—some from the FAA (Federal Aviation Administration), others probably from the CIA (Central Intelligence Agency). The copilot, who had been the one to photograph the UFO, received his camera back with no film in it. Two days after they signed several papers and were sworn to secrecy, a very serious, elderly gentleman with wide-awake eyes made something abundantly clear to them: "The event never happened," he said. "Keep that in mind for your entire life. You were victims of a mirage of lights emanating from the planet Mars." The FAA's subsequent investigative report stated that the whole incident was due to a radar malfunction. The device had created a "shared blip."

PSEUDOSCIENCE WITHOUT END

About fifty years ago, the American biologist Dr. Strauss of Johns Hopkins University declared that the snowman called Yeti was nothing more than a polar bear. "Since our hypothesis is the only non-fantastic assumption, it must be true."[1] According to this logic, all you have to do now is notify the Yeti that he is a polar bear.

Although I have never had the opportunity to experience a clear UFO sighting, I have been able to speak with very serious, often shocked people about their respective UFO experiences. Most witnesses suffer silently because those who try to defend the UFO issue in this world are simply considered "stupid."[2] Serious people are not concerned with it. That's it! And the few who try to explain their experiences land on the rubbish heap of ridicule. They are forcefully expelled from the company of the serious. TV programs such as *The Truth about UFOs* show alleged spectacular UFO sightings that are then unequivocally refuted immediately thereafter by pseudo-serious smart alecks.[3]

The message is always clear: UFO witnesses are idiots across the board. At which institute does one have to study to become a UFO researcher, for example? At the same one where rabbit breeders, egg sellers, and shaving-brush manufacturers enroll—that is, no such institute exists. At which institute do you have to enroll to participate in a study group geared toward refuting UFO researchers? The same one! Thus, people with equal rights face each other, but the significant difference is that the anti-UFO lobby always wins.

Whoever has seen UFOs, whoever has even had the misfortune to suffer an "encounter of the third kind," is, without objective proof, left out in the rain. And even if good photos or a mobile phone video substantiate an experience, such evidence isn't valid. It's all computer generated we are told with a raised index finger. If even 50, 100, or 1000 people describe the same UFO event, they are victims of mass suggestion. They observed a mirage or the parts of rockets or satellites that continuously crash into our atmosphere all over the world, 365 days a year.

So basically UFOs are a never-ending bombardment of earthly garbage from space. And if no trick can conjure up space debris, UFOs turn out to be lightweight aircraft, children's kites, hot air balloons, reflections, hallucinations, inventions and fantasies, mosquito swarms, high-flying weather balloons, headlight reflections, or brightly glowing planets, which race with insane speeds around the earth at night. The anti-UFO lobby, pseudoscientific through and through, is always attached to the mantle of science; it uses methods of denigration and exclusion and asserts its "seriousness" at every inappropriate opportunity. This is a society you want to run away from.

But how does this ignorant and knowledge-hating society behave in terms of verifiable cases when the issue is not just a play of lights, but when people were taken inside strange objects? I am aware of several such "encounters of the fourth kind," and I only talk about them because I have personally met the participants.

A POTENTIAL TIME MACHINE AND A BAFFLED SHERIFF

In the early evening of October 11, 1973, two factory workers in Pascagoula, Mississippi, were taken inside a large, colored sphere and examined by strangers. Pascagoula is a small town in southern Mississippi, part of Jackson County. It is known for its Northrop Grumman Ship Systems (NGSS) shipyards. Until 2006, the US Navy also maintained a shipyard in Pascagoula.

So what happened that evening?

Charles (Charly) Hickson and Calvin Parker worked outside the factory halls on a site where metal pieces of all sizes and alloys were stored directly on the Pascagoula River. One evening, the two were fishing near their work site when, out of nowhere, a sphere rose up over the plant. The two workers became dizzy; their knees became weak. Two creatures in glowing suits pushed them into the sphere. Once inside, they were pressed against a wall, and strange devices moved slowly over their bodies. After this peculiar investigation, both were gently carried back outside and placed on a large metal plate. The case has been investigated by all conceivable authorities.[4]

FIGURE 1.1: *Charles Hickson*

I met the two victims on November 27, 1973, in a hotel in Pascagoula. At the time, Calvin was a young lad, just nineteen years old. He seemed reserved, and let his older colleague, Charly do the talking.

"Where did the sphere come from?" I asked. "Did you see it approach in flight?"

Charly responded: "We were using a forklift to stack smaller steel girders. It was 4:30 pm and we were just talking about a new car Calvin had bought. Suddenly it seemed as if somebody hit my ears with both hands at the same time. The same happened to my colleague.

"Perplexed, we turned around and saw something shimmering above the water of the Pascagoula River that changed its colors from glaring white to blue, violet, yellow, and then reddish. Out of this, a sphere emerged; I estimated its height to be eight meters. I wanted to scream and run, but it was like a dream. We both were somehow paralyzed. Surprised, we noticed how a crack formed on the sphere from which a glaring light emanated. Then two little creatures floated toward us in something like white overalls. They had big eyes, no hair or helmets, but where the nostrils should be, there was something indefinable. The two reached under our underarms, touched us lightly, and then we floated with them over the pieces of metal on the ground. I panicked, I wanted to run away, but no muscle moved. I was paralyzed like I was under anesthesia. I looked over at Calvin. He was completely pale, his skin was waxy, and his eyes were closed. As we floated through the gap into the interior of the sphere, I too had to close my eyes, because the light blinded me like a stadium light would do. I felt [myself] being gently pushed against a wall and was terribly scared. Any moment now, I thought, they would kill me. But the wall tipped slowly into a sloping position. I smelled something that I cannot describe, because there is no comparable odor. Then I realized that I could move my arms and pressed the backs of my hands on both eyes. Something went across my face; I only registered it by the shadow that passed over my closed eyes. Now the wall tipped back into the vertical position and I felt very faintly the pressure of my body on my feet. Because of the bright light, I did not dare open my eyes. Again I realized that I was floating, and at the same time I heard the traffic from the highway bridge. We were outside again. Now I opened my eyes, saw the two strangers with their big eyes drop us on a metal plate and float back to their sphere. The color of the sphere changed again as it had done at the beginning of the spectacle, then it took on a glaring white light, and then it disappeared. I straightened up, squatted, letting my legs dangle from the metal plate, and look[ed] for the sphere on the horizon. But there was nothing. I told Calvin, who was lying next to me, that he should not be afraid anymore and [to] open his eyes. At the same time, we heard the sirens of a police car. Then, two sheriffs stormed toward us."

"Where did the police car come from?" I asked.

Charly explained that to the left of his workplace was a wide bridge over the Pascagoula River. The sheriff had driven across the bridge with his deputy and, quite irritated, had looked at the lightshow that the sphere had set up *beneath* them. They wanted to investigate, but it was only possible to reach the yard in front of the hangar by driving to the next highway exit and approaching the yard from the opposite direction. As a result, it took the sheriff six minutes to reach the place, at the same time the strangers laid their two victims on the metal plank. The sheriff and his deputy did witness the colored lights and sphere and were able to observe how it dissolved into nothing. Later, another eighteen eyewitnesses came forward to say they had seen the spectacle with the sphere from the other side of the river.

FIGURE 1.2: *On the left, the bridge over the Pascagoula River over which the sheriff came*

What happened here? No power on Earth currently (or in the 70s) possesses such technologies. Are we perhaps dealing with time travelers? And a sphere that changes colors and then disappears? If you can think, you should be a responsible thinker.

Doctors tried to classify the case of Pascagoula psychologically. But categorizing this as a psychological variant is just another excuse to fool us and lull us. The zealots, who expose everything that has anything to do with extraterrestrial and other inexplicable phenomena to ridicule, have already done too much mischief. The claims that all such experiences are just common-sense occurrences are nothing more than presumptuousness. Of all people, it is disappointing for scientists to behave pseudo-scientifically and block us from gaining knowledge.

THE NEVER-ENDING CASE OF B. AND B. HILL AND A VISIT FROM ZETA RETICULI

In this chapter, I examine some related stories that nobody knows about. Those who were affected entrusted their statements to me. One such story is the case of Barney and Betty Hill. For those familiar with the literature, feeling the influence of an unknown power is a well-known story. Several books have been written about it, and I have also dealt with this particular case in detail.[5] In my earlier description of this case, however, I did not reveal my long conversation with Betty Hill.

So assuming you are not familiar with the story, let me first provide a short version of this well-documented case.

—

At the time this story took place, the night of September 19 and 20, 1961, Betty and Barney Hill were returning from a holiday in Canada to their home in Portsmouth, New Hampshire. Betty was forty-two and Barney was a thirty-nine-year old post office worker. Just before midnight, on US Route 3 (Daniel Webster Highway), they noticed a bright object moving rapidly over the southwestern sky. Barney stopped several times so they could take a closer look at the crazy light.

South of Indian Head in the White Mountains, and 2.3 miles north of Woodstock, the strange object raced silently toward Barney and Betty Hill's car, blocking their onward journey. Barney stopped and got out, still firmly convinced that the US Air Force was trying something new and they just happened to be witnessing it.

Then the UFO changed position and slid slowly toward the stationary car . . .

Some time passed. It was quiet in the car. Barney and Betty looked at the passing scenery and wondered where they were. Their minds seemed to tell them somehow that they had slept or been absent for a while. Both spoke little, both were thinking. They drove past Concord and took Exit 4 toward the ocean and Portsmouth. The birds were already chirping and the houses shone in the gray morning light as they drove through Portsmouth. That seemed impossible, because according to their schedule, they should have been home already; they were supposed to have arrived around 4:00 am. Strangely enough, both their watches had stopped. When they got home and sat down at the kitchen table, the two of them realizing that they were missing over two hours of memory and thirty-five miles of driving . . .

—

Sixteen years later, February 23, 1977, I met widowed Betty Hill (Barney died in 1969). At the time, Betty was fifty-seven, very modest, amiable, and correct. With a deep inner conviction, she described her experience that night. She had still not come to terms with the event, which became clear during our conversation.

Betty said she was tired of having to tell the same story over and over again, especially because of the way hypocritical and all-knowing critics had treated her countless times.

"Betty," I said, "I'm not here to denounce you in any way. I definitely know that aliens exist. But I would be grateful to hear about the experience directly from you."

Betty started talking about how, after the incident, they met and entrusted themselves to well-known Boston psychiatrist Dr. Benjamin Simon and how she allowed him to hypnotize her. The doctor had treated the couple separately and had recorded tapes during the sessions, which he then played back to both of them. Bit by bit, like a jigsaw puzzle, their memories of the missing two hours returned.

"Was the unknown object spherical?" I wanted to know.

"Not quite," Betty replied. "My husband estimated the object to be 25 to 30 feet high and lightly dented at both ends like some kind of pancake. It had something like transparent hatches and the light was coming from them."

She then told me that two groups of small creatures with oversized eyes, small nostrils, and small mouths approached their car and led the two of them inside the strange object. The strangers wore dark, leathery, tight-fitting clothes. One of them said, in heavily accented English—she said it sounded like the way people in India speak—that they did not have to worry, that nothing was going to happen to them.

"You did not resist?" I asked.

"We were shocked and were moving obediently, like remote-controlled puppets," she replied.

Inside the object, Betty Hill said, she was first placed on a white chair and then asked to lie down comfortably on a lounger. There the creatures moved their fingers through her hair, and touched her eyes, ears, and fingertips. Several of the strangers, conversing in a sort of chant in subdued higher tones, had been in the room.

"Did you recognize any of the interior design?"

Betty said, "The room was round and reminded me of a wedding cake with a massive pillar in the middle. The English-speaking entity held something like a camera with an oversized lens in his hands. Then the one I now refer to as the doctor took some kind of ruler and scratched my arm with it. Later, he pressed something slightly sticky, like cellophane, on my chest and pulled it off again. Finally, he took a thin needle and slid it into my bellybutton. That hurt. The doctor noticed this and put his hand briefly on my left temple. Instantly the pain was gone."

"At last," Betty reported without emotion, "the beings left the room. Only the one who spoke English stayed. I felt very relieved, because the examination seemed to be over. I asked the remaining being where their home was. The extraterrestrial waved with one hand, and a three-dimensional, colored star chart appeared on a wall. The stranger said that our solar system is also part of this section. Then he said something, sarcastically—that it was pointless to show me where they came from because I would not even know which position our sun took in this chart. I looked at the dotted tangle and then asked him what the lines meant, connecting the larger stars to the smaller ones. The stranger said that the information was of no use to me, but that it indicated trade and research routes but also planets that had been colonized with new life forms.

Then two other creatures led Barney into the room. They conversed again in their chant and then led us back outside. In the dim moonlight, I saw our car with its doors torn open. Barney wanted to get behind the wheel, but a heavy wrench was in his seat. When we came to our senses, we were on the highway just before Concord. The wrench was now in the back seat. Barney could not remember ever having held it in his hand . . ."

—

This concludes the main part of the interview I recorded with Betty Hill. But the case became much more complicated. Critics accused the two of having told a story of lies, that they had nightmares, that they lacked evidence, that everything was too farfetched, that the aliens were way too human, and that all their descriptions could be explained as being psychologically plausible. A psychologist attested to a fictional memory, and the smart alecks of the repression faction even proclaimed that the Hill couple had been fooled that night by planet Jupiter. As it usually is with other similar cases over the decades, arguments and counterarguments abounded.[6] Each party was able to choose according to their wishes.

During hypnosis sessions, however, Betty Hill told of the three-dimensional star map and traced that map from memory. Later this happened twice more under post-hypnotic influence. Every time, she created the same drawing. Two images had stuck in Betty's memory: an isosceles triangle at the lower-left edge of the picture and two larger, side-by-side spheres connected by several strands. The fact that these images were constant over all her experiences is what made an expert take up the issue.

—

Marjorie Fish, astronomer and member of *Mensa International,* saw Betty's drawing in an astronomical journal. The two ladies met on August 4, 1969. Ms. Fish built several models that could be observed from all angles. Lo and behold, the nut was cracked. Everything was right: the distances between the stars, the three stars in the isosceles triangle at the lower left, and the two consecutive main stars connected by lines. And what really seemed impossible was this: Betty Hill had drawn a constellation that included stars, some of which were first published in the 1969 Gliese Star Chart. Before 1969, apart from astronomer Wilhelm Gliese and a few experts in astronomy, no one knew anything about this constellation. Betty Hill first drew her chart in 1964, five years before the publication of the Gliese catalog.

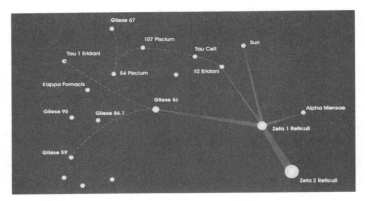

FIGURE 1.3: The star chart drawn by Betty Hill

Astronomer Dr. Allen Hynek commented: "All [of] this is fascinating and inexplicable. No astronomer in the world knew between 1961 and 1964 of the triangle constellation that Betty Hill had drawn under hypnosis as a geometric star position."[7]

Of course, constant attempts are made to cast doubt on Betty's star chart. Thanks to the Hubble telescope, we now know much more about the celestial region in question than we did at the time Betty Hill's story took place. Today, we know of additional stars that did not show up on the Hill map. Correct. But that does not change the result. As early as 1969, astronomer Marjorie Fish had many more stars in the Gliese catalog than Betty Hill had on her chart.

But even then, all the heavenly bodies were eliminated on which no life could exist—for example, white dwarfs, red giants, or double suns.

Do we know now where the strangers came from? From the star system Zeta 1 + 2 and Reticuli. The celestial bodies are about thirty-seven light-years away from us, which basically tells you everything about the space technology of those foreign visitors.

——

The cases cited here, that of Kenju Terauchi, Calvin Parker/Charly Hickson, and Barney and Betty Hill, are not stories I have simply taken from UFO literature. I knew all the participants and am convinced of the authenticity of their descriptions. It is not just their spoken words, but also their feelings of helplessness and the extreme emotions they all exhibited. Unfortunately, some groups in our society do not want to know about all the UFO encounters and, according to their logic, do their best to refute such events. I call these groups the *repression faction*. But even though the repression faction cannot provide scientifically sound evidence for their assumptions, these assumptions often too quickly become alleged counterevidence. "The Hill case has long since then been refuted," I read. No, it has not. Those who refute it only conjured up other assumptions from their box of desired outcomes. In the case of Barney and Betty Hill hard facts were pushed away—for example, the large, round, coin-shaped stains on the roof of Barney's car.

A DESPERATE NICK POPE

During the night of December 27, 1980, an unknown light appeared above the military base of the Royal Air

Force in Bentwaters, UK. The thing then shone ever brighter, morphed into a small pyramid, and sunk into a grove of trees beyond the airbase's fence. Sergeant Jim Penniston led a small party to the lights. The party measured and touched the pyramid; they found it to be about 2.7 meters wide and 2 meters tall. It then slowly rose to the height of the treetops and moved away at incredible speed. When it was gone, the party could see that upon entering the grove, the light-emitting pyramid object had broken branches and left impressions in the icy winter ground.

=

I received all information about this event from Nick Pope. Nick worked for the British Department of Defense from 1985 to 2006 and was head of the official British UFO office.

When I interviewed him, Nick confirmed "That's one of the perfectly documented cases."

"What do the skeptics think?" I asked.

Nick Pope ran his fingers through his hair, looked me in the eye, shrugged his shoulders in despair, and shook his head helplessly.

"For them, the case has long since been refuted. It was the reflective light of a lighthouse."

To me, something like that sounds like complete nonsense. The reflectors of that lighthouse threw their rays into the area night after night and had done so for decades. In addition, lights do not bend branches or leave impressions on frozen ground. For how long can the world's population and powerful journalists be deceived and kept quiet by such nonsensical statements? And what about all this sad posturing in the name of science, in the name of "common sense?" It is simply horrifying!

A PROFESSOR WITH CIVIC COURAGE: A VISIT FROM THE FATHER OF SPACE TRAVEL

The icing on the cake was provided by John Mack, with whom I was allowed to talk extensively and privately on multiple occasions. But who is John Mack, and what is this all about?

Twenty-five years ago, American author Budd Hopkins presented the results of a multiyear study he had conducted with the aid of several US scientists.[8] Hopkins claimed that individual human beings had been abducted by aliens and even wore alien implants. The scientific response to Hopkins' revelations was consistent. Kidnapped by aliens? All nonsense!

In the following years, several publications appeared on the same topic.[9] Public opinion, however, didn't change at all. In the German-speaking world, these publications were followed by the very-well-documented work of Dr. Johannes Fiebag on abducted humans, which was published without any significant reaction from society.[10] It was then that Professor John E. Mack came out with a book that bore the stunning title *Abductions*.[11] Mack could no longer be ignored. He was not just a professor of psychiatry and medicine at one of America's most prestigious colleges—Harvard University in Cambridge, Massachusetts—but he was also a bearer of the coveted Pulitzer Prize. Mack's answer to his scientific colleagues and to all the skeptics in the world was staggering: the result of his research was that abduction victims were not crazy; semen samples had been taken from several men, artificial insemination had taken place, and none of this could be described as merely fantastical thinking by the victims.

I knew Professor Mack pretty well. We spoke at the same conferences and also had private discussions. Mack was disappointed with public reactions, especially in scientific journals. He said people being kidnapped by UFOs was too whacky a thought, too much for our minds to accept. Scientists and journalists, who generally don't believe in UFOs, cannot be convinced by facts. The brain refuses—represses—uncomfortable truths. Skeptics know the usual arguments against UFOs, they *know* with sleepwalking certainty that there are no UFOs, *that they just can't exist.* This indoctrinated shield is perfect—the brain blocks out information that doesn't fit its narrative completely. And people who, to some extent, can still come to terms with UFOs consider kidnapping grotesque, a fantasy, and completely wrong. They see no reason for aliens to behave in such a way, if they exist at all.

"Are you completely convinced that people were actually kidnapped by UFOs?" I asked Professor Mack in a restaurant in Istanbul.

"We are all participants in a universe teeming with intelligent life forms from which we have cut ourselves off," Mack replied. "We are being watched, and there have been kidnappings. Even though I do not like it at all. I hate to be watched, and, even more, hate to be treated like an animal in a zoological garden by a strange intelligence."

"But the evidence is missing," I ventured to say.

"It's not missing at all," Mack replied, and I heard some mockery and bitterness in his voice. "Isolated victims wore implants. We have surgically removed and investigated them. We didn't find any elements that can't also be found somewhere on Earth. But we could not make sense of the composition."

"I don't quite understand . . ."

"We humans tag bears, dolphins, or wolves to calculate their travel routes. A bear may like to see and sniff the tag on another bear. But it cannot understand what it is for."

"And why do we not read anything about such implants in the media? Wouldn't that be sensational!"

"Erich—what are you thinking? The time is not yet ripe for this." Mack said.

Meanwhile, images of implants have been published again and again; for example, in *Ergebnisse aus 40 Jahren UFO-Forschung (Results from 40 Years of UFO Research)* by astrophysicist Illobrand von Ludwiger.[12] The ignorant skeptics' circus only makes him yawn.

Nonsensical conspiracy theories? Only the fantasies of idiotic people who want to make themselves seem important? Nothing behind it but lots of blabber?

As the science journalist Leslie Kean has proven, the US government issued clear guidelines as early as 1953, when UFO sightings became fashionable, in order to ridicule these things:

> *All intelligence agencies are required to influence the mass media and infiltrate civilian research groups for the purpose of disparaging the idea of UFOs ... to treat UFO reports as untrustworthy and ridiculous ... The public interest in UFO incidents should be undermined and diminished . . . and intelligence agents should ensure that the facts are withheld from leading investigators through targeted disinformation.*

All these recommendations were recorded in black and white by the explosive CIA *Robertson Panel Report*, which wasn't made public until 1975.[13]

So you say there are no conspiracy theories? Was not this a CIA conspiracy against UFO witnesses? The intelligence of humans has been assaulted for decades. But the intelligentsia is still struggling to understand that it has been abused and purposefully deceived.

=

About 25 years ago, Dr. J. Allen Hynek, a professor of astronomy, I, and a few others were guests on a US talk show. One of the participants said to Professor Hynek: "If there were any intelligent species out there watching us, they would long have had diplomatic relations with us."

Allen Hynek replied, "We do not have any diplomatic relations with chickens."

—

I know of similarly hard-hitting remarks from the "father of space exploration," Dr. Hermann Oberth (1894–1989). He and his daughter had been guests at Hotel Rosenhügel in Davos, Switzerland, several times, a hotel I used to manage. He had smiled and read my then-unpublished manuscript, *Erinnerungen an die Zukunft (Chariots of the Gods)*, saying, "the upcoming criticism must run off you like manure off a marble pillar." Oberth also told me how he had gotten involved in space travel. As a young man, an engineer by profession, he had read Jules Verne's book *From Earth to the Moon*. In it, Verne (1828–1905), the master of science fiction, told of three people who were shot to the moon in a hollow cannonball. "That's never going to work," young Hermann Oberth had objected and he began to calculate. What energy would be necessary to overcome the gravitational pull? In 1923 his groundbreaking book *Die Raketezu den Planetenräumen (The Rocket to the Planetary Spaces)* was published. With Oberth's formulas, a journey through space suddenly moved into the realm of the possible. And, oddly enough, during the Second World War, the same Hermann Oberth taught Wernher von Braun (1912–1977). Wernher von Braun, in turn, tinkered in Peenemünde on Hitler's "miracle weapon," the V-2. Toward the end of the war, von Braun defected to the US and with the *Apollo 11* mission, in July 1969, he successfully carried out that shot to the moon.

This is an excellent example of how fantasy becomes reality. There was just one generation between the visionary Jules Verne and the realizer Wernher von Braun. But the impulse came from Jules Verne, the visionary.

—

In our time, and I type these lines in the summer of 2015, rumors continue to emerge that the Nazis developed UFOs and that some of the engineers managed to escape to Argentina, that they built underground bases there, and that all UFOs were really nothing other than Nazi developments. Even the History Channel spreads this Nazi nonsense in its otherwise quite reasonable series *Ancient Aliens*.

The rumors about Nazi UFOs already existed by the late 1960s. I discussed this with Professor Hermann Oberth.

"Did you develop UFOs in secrecy?" I said.

"Yes, we worked on it," Oberth, the father of space travel, said slowly. "But we did not make any breakthroughs. Mission-ready UFOs—Germany would not have lost World War II." That hit hard!

A MOVIE FROM THE COCKPIT

Those currently in control will never admit the existence of UFOs. I am already chuckling about the "repudiations" of the following case.

—

In agreement with the Puerto Rican authorities, Americans were conducting reconnaissance flights against drug smugglers in Puerto Rican airspace. At 1:22 pm, on April 26, 2013, an unknown object appeared on the radar of an American border control aircraft.

Firmly installed in the cockpit of the US aircraft is a camera that records all flight movements and displays all data in real time. The following information is provided around the edge of the screen: north-south direction, the longitude and latitude of the aircraft position, the exact heading and altitude of the aircraft, the aircraft's altitude above ground, its heading (0 to 360 degrees) from the crosshair, the distance of the aircraft from its target, the longitude and latitude of the target, the exact time (to the nearest second), and the speed of both the aircraft and the target. All of this data is updated and displayed in tenths of a second. It is an integral part of the recordings from the cockpit. The pilot cannot change any of this.

The black object first appeared to the right of the crosshairs of the target viewfinder. The pilot caught it again, tracked it, lost it briefly, and then caught it again. You could almost get the impression that this UFO wanted to be filmed because as soon as its speed became too high, it changed shape and slowed down. The UFO flew over meadows and fields, then over the Rafael Hernandez Airport TJBQ at Aguadilla, which promptly closed for takeoffs and landings.

The object flew at incredible speed over two ships at the seaport and then dove directly into the water of the Atlantic Ocean.

The spraying fountains created by the impact reconfirmed the material form of the UFO. A second later, two objects emerged from the water.

—

I make the following pictures public here and do not doubt that the sectarians of truth denouncement will conjure up a gigantic fakery. Or they will be silent. The ingenious physicist and Nobel Laureate Max Planck once said that every single serious finding goes through three phases: 1) Everyone denies it; 2) Everyone is shamefully silent; and then 3) Everyone shouts: We've always told you so!

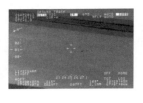

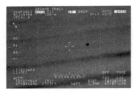

FIGURE 1.4: UFO over Puerto Rico; these pictures were taken on April 26, 2013, from the cockpit of a US fighter jet.

CHAPTER 2

Fairytales for Christians

In which you will learn about the following:

Encounters in Kashmir • Language Cultures •
A Shock for All Christians: No Ascension •
The Jesus Grave • The Invented Original Texts •
Old Indian Vedas

ENCOUNTERS IN KASHMIR

On October 23, 1974, I received a letter from Dr. F. M. Hassnain from Kashmir, India. I did not know anything about him, but I learned from the letterhead that he was a scholar employed in the Kashmir State Archives. I learned more about him through later correspondence.[1] Dr. Hassnain served as Chief of Archives, but he also lectured for the Kashmir Research Center for Buddhist Studies (KRCBS) in Srinagar. He wrote that he had read two of my books and that he thought his home country should be of great interest to me. Not only are there enigmatic ruins from a bygone era in the highlands of Kashmir, but there is also the tomb of Jesus, the founder of the Christian religion.

At first I was stunned. The unknown ruins interested me, but Jesus's grave could not exist anywhere. I was raised Catholic and know the New Testament, and it states that Jesus rose from the dead and ascended into heaven. So Jesus has no grave. I wrote all of this to my new contact. But he replied that he knew the Gospels as well as I did and that our knowledge of Jesus was incomplete—and that he could prove it. But to do so, he would need me to travel to Srinagar. As head of the archives, he could show me old documents and the 2000-year-old Jesus grave.

—

Srinagar is located at what seems to be the end of the world in the highlands of India, near Tibet. (I described the adventurous path I took to reach Kashmir in one of my previous books.[2])

I met Dr. Hassnain on the terrace of the Oberoi Inn Hotel in Srinagar. This spacious building has terraces, park-like gardens, and fountains and is located on Wular Lake. Srinagar is also known as the Venice of Asia because it is crisscrossed by many canals that are teeming with boats, gondolas, and anchored houseboats. Srinagar is on the thirty-forth parallel, just like Gibraltar and Damascus. As a result, you would think

FIGURE 2.1: *Srinagar in the highlands of Kashmir*

that it should really be hot there, but because of its altitude, 1730 meters above sea level, the climate is very pleasant.

Dr. Hassnain, a bald, friendly man of medium height, greeted me the customary Indian way, by placing his arms in front of his chest with his palms pressed together and giving a slight nod. A second man stood next to him—Dr. R. K. Koul, a Sanskrit scholar and the assistant director for the *State Gazetteers*, a state publication. After the courtesies, I got straight to the point:

"Professor, Jesus's grave does not exist. Jesus ascended to heaven."

He smiled good-naturedly and said, "You will not be able to resist the evidence."

"What evidence? I am capable of learning," I replied.

LANGUAGE CULTURES

"I assume," Hassnain began, "that during your car ride through our country, you observed how similar the local population is to the people of historic Palestine. They are of the same stature, have the same almond eyes, and similar noses. The boys are circumcised here as well. As in ancient Palestine, the dead are buried in an east-west direction. And as in Israel today, the men in Kashmir wear their *kippah,* the little cap, on the back of their heads. Our national language has countless similarities with the oldest branch of the Western Semitic language, the language that Jesus and his disciples spoke."

FIGURE 2.2: *As in Israel, the men in Kashmir wear kippahs on their heads.*

"Do you have any examples?" I was interested. Dr. Hassnain reached for a paper napkin and on it, he wrote a few words below and next to each other:

ARAMAIC	KASCHMIRI	MEANING
A kh	akh	alone
Ajal	ajal	death
Awa	awan	blind
Ahad	ahad	one
Hamah	humaham	noise
Loal	lol	love
Qatal	qatal	killer
Qabar	qabar	grave

Carefully, and in a tone devoid of any righteousness, he continued: "An old Kashmiri tradition says that the exodus of the Israelites did not lead them for forty years through the Sinai desert, but through the present-day countries of Jordan, Syria, Persia, Afghanistan, and Pakistan, and finally to the highlands of India. This explains the various struggles the Israelites were exposed to during their migration. They had to fight their way through. That did not happen in Sinai. Here, in this country, are located Moses's tomb and the gardens of Solomon, and here are the mountains mentioned in Deuteronomy, which you seek in vain in Palestine. Believe me, Mr. von Däniken—and I will prove it in the state archives—when Jesus came here after his alleged death, he did not seek a vague destination, he wanted to go to the *Land of the Fathers!*"

"And how did Jesus know about this land?" I asked.

"Oral traditions and written references were found a few decades ago in the Dead Sea Scrolls. There is also an unknown period of time in the life of Jesus. Nobody knows where he was between the ages of twelve and thirty. Maybe he spent some years of his youth here."

"Excuse me," I interjected, "he would have had to travel about 4000 kilometers to come here. How would he have done that?"

It was then that Dr. Koul joined the conversation. "Think of the Canadian settlers," he said. "Without railroads, airplanes, or cars, they made the journey from the East to the West Coast of North America with their families and covered wagons in nine months. And that was a distance of 7000 kilometers!"

I admit that this conversation confused my thoughts. It was all hard to digest. Although I had long ago developed well-founded doubts about the biblical account of Jesus, what I heard here completely contradicted the history of Jewry and Christianity. Where was the evidence? And what about the old documents that Dr. Hassnain had mentioned? I was about to find out.

―

The next day the three of us drove to the *Takht-i-Suleiman,* the Throne of Solomon, on a hilltop near Srinagar. At the ruins of a temple wall, Dr. Hassnain showed me two inscriptions in a written type that I could not read. He translated: "During this time the

Prophet Yusu preached." And below it, "It is Yus Asaf, the prophet of the children of Israel."

Yus, so I learned, was the translation for the word *Jesus.* In the library of the Kashmir State Archives, a gray building from the British colonial era, Dr. Hassnain gathered some books and slides that I could again not decipher. Everything had been neatly written in Sanskrit with a pointy pen.

Hassnain began speaking: "This writing is entitled *Bhavishya Maha Purana.* From pages 465 to 467, an encounter between Jesus and the former ruler of Kashmir is recorded. The city was founded by King Pravayasena, but at the time of Jesus, Raya Shalewahin ruled. I translate the text:

> *During the reign of Raya Shalewahin, the ruler had himself carried over the cool hills of Kashmir. Then the king saw a happy person in white linen sitting in the grass and around him several others who listened to him. Shalewahin sat down and asked the stranger who he was. The man in the white robe answered calmly, "I was born of a young woman. I am the preacher of the Mlachha religion of true principles."*

> *The king continued, "What is this religion?"*

> *The stranger answered: "Omaharay [great ruler], I walked and preached in the country of Mlachha [geographically Palestine] and taught the truths and taught against the destruction of traditions. I appeared there and they called me Masih [Messiah]. The rulers there did not like my teachings, they rejected the traditions and condemned me. I suffered a lot at their hands."*

When the king wanted to know more about the foreign religion, the man in white linen answered: "Religion means love, truth, and purity of the heart. That's why I was called Masih."

I was confused. Dr. Hassnain smiled at me and asked if he could translate the other scriptures. Since I could not read anything anyway, I declined. "Maybe tomorrow," I said. "Please, dear professor, explain to me how a crucified, supposedly dead Jesus came to Kashmir."

A SHOCK FOR ALL CHRISTIANS: NO ASCENSION

We sat down in an office where we were served sweet black tea.

"Christians believe Jesus died on the cross. That is a misconception. Jesus was crucified on a Friday at lunchtime. Friday at sunset, the Sabbath began, the seventh day of the week, the day of rest and spiritual renewal. The Roman occupiers did not care about the local religions. Everyone could believe in as many gods as they wanted, and they respected the religious laws of their subjects. Therefore no one was allowed to remain hanging on the cross on the Sabbath. Historians like the Roman Flavius Josephus, a contemporary of Jesus, have stated that the crucifixion punishment was not necessarily a death sentence, but a barbaric torture that could be survived by someone with a strong and healthy body . . ."

"But ..." I interrupted, "... in the New Testament, it says a Roman soldier stabbed Jesus in the side and blood and water flowed out ..."

"... proving that Jesus was not dead. Had he been dead, no blood circulation would have been possible. But let's look at it step by step: In the presence of some women, Joseph and Nicodemus were allowed to take the body off the cross. The clever men had the crucifixion guards, who were already drinking wine at this time of day, believing that the Lord was dead. The women went along with this charade, covered his wounded body with cloths, and then they most likely took Jesus to the house of Nicodemus, a rich man. There he was treated with ointments and herbs and, when he was ready to be moved, they carted him to the Essene monastery at the Dead Sea. Remember, Mr. von Däniken, from the Dead Sea Scrolls we know that Jesus himself had grown up among the Essenes. This conservative community raised boys without parents. Several passages in the New Testament, which we now clearly know were not spoken by Jesus for the first time, were part of the teachings of the Essenes. . . .

"Excuse me?" I said and stared at Professor Hassnain in disbelief.

"Take the famous Sermon on the Mount. The Beatitudes in it were not invented by the divine mind of Jesus; they already existed in the teachings of the Essenes. The announcements of a Kingdom of heaven? Part of the Essenes.

"The announcements of a great judgement? Part of the Essenes. There are many ideas in the New Testament that can be found before Jesus in other religions. Often these were adopted word for word from other texts. [I published a comparison in *Erscheinungen*.[3]] John the Baptist and Jesus, by the way, grew up in the same monastery school."

"But there was clearly a grave of Jesus!" I interjected.

"This grave belonged to wealthy Nicodemus. Maybe it was reserved for him. The Evangelist Luke . . . ," at this point Professor Hassnain picked up the Bible, " . . . describes in chapter 24 verse 1 of his gospel how two young men wanted to visit the tomb of Jesus. But the women answered, 'Why are you looking for the living among the dead?'"

At this point, Dr. Aziz Kashmiri, the author of a book about Jesus, stepped into the room. Dr. Hassnain invited him to sit down. Dr. Kashmiri knew everything about the gospels and the life of Jesus. He offered to take me to the tomb of Jesus the next day, but I was not ready for that. Our discussion became more heated:

"The New Testament describes how Jesus ascended into heaven. There can be no grave of him. Certainly not here," I added mockingly.

The slender Dr. Kashmiri, who seemed to be nothing but skin and bones, looked inquisitively at Dr. Hassnain. The professor nodded. Kashmiri opened two different English Bibles in front of me. Certain passages were highlighted.

"Mr. von Däniken," he began in a quiet baritone, "I really don't want to instill religious doubts . . ."

"I have had those since . . ."

"Look here, the Gospel of Matthew, chapter 28 verses 16 and 17," Dr. Kashmiri lectured me. "Jesus commanded his disciples to climb a mountain in Galilee. When they saw him, they threw themselves down. 'Some were doubtful.' Still? Even though he stood physically before them? Matthew has nothing more to say about an Ascension. And Mark, in chapter 16 verse 19, writes just one sentence about the miraculous event: "The Lord Jesus, after speaking to them, was lifted up to heaven and sat down at the right hand of God." As if he had been there! In Luke, on the other hand, Jesus personally leads his disciples 'towards Bethany.' As he blessed them, he 'departed from them and rose to heaven.' Still missing is the favorite disciple, John. The one who, at the Last Supper, was leaning against Jesus's chest. Amazing—he does not know anything about an Ascension . . . ."

I began to feel very uneasy. I was educated the same way as many hundreds of millions of Catholics, I spent a full five years in a Jesuit boarding school, I had had to translate Bible excerpts in Greek and Latin, and now I sat in a neon-lit room in front of an empty teacup in the highlands of India listening to two scholars who were about to destroy what remained of my faith. Why did the evangelists have contradictory opinions on the Ascension? After all, they had all been there in person and should have described the phenomenal event in a unified way. Why did Jesus's favorite disciple John not know about it? This grandiose experience should not only have been a sensation to all present, but also to the uninvolved audience. Actually, all of Jerusalem should have talked about such an event. But not a single Jewish or Roman historian of the time noted a word about it.

Carefully, I ventured another objection: "Why an Ascension at all? You do not just invent a supernatural event like that."

"And you in particular, Mr. von Däniken, why are you asking about it?" Dr. Hassnain laughed. "From your research you know that an ascension was something the people at that time considered quite possible. In your books, you bring a lot of evidence for gods who went to heaven—I mean to say, into outer space. Biblical figures like Enoch or Elijah have gone to heaven. That was known to the people! Gods always resided in the sky. For the writers of the New Testament, Jesus could never be worth less than the earlier gods or prophets. They *had to* conjure up an ascension. That's why there are these contradictions!"

"And how did this undead Jesus, who did not ascend to heaven, come to the highlands of Kashmir?"

As he kept leafing through some of the books, Dr. Hassnain provided the answer:

"After Jesus was well again, he showed himself to his disciples in hidden places. Thomas did not want to believe it even then. Jesus allowed him to touch his crucifixion wounds. But the Roman state power

heard through the rumor mill that the crucified Naza-
rene had apparently reappeared. Jesus himself could
not show himself anywhere. His face was known in
the city. Probably his teachers from the monastery of
the Essenes advised him to walk to the highlands of
Kashmir. And in any case, his tribal members lived
there."

At this point, I thought: In fact, Jesus could not
have hidden in any country west of Israel. The entire
Mediterranean was then part of the Roman Empire.
Only an escape eastward promised safety from Roman
persecutors. I remembered the story of Saul, a clever
Roman officer. He must have had similar thoughts,
because he set a trap for Jesus near today's Damascus.
"Saul, Saul, why do you persecute me?" (Acts 9:4)

"It must have come to a conversation between
Jesus and Saul," said Dr. Kashmiri. "Jesus convinced
his pursuer to let him go. Never forget, Mr. von Däniken, that Saul called himself Paul from that point on. It
was Paul, not Jesus, who spread the new religion. Jesus
taught that, before God, all men are equal. But this con-
cept was highly political. Should slaves and their kin
be worth the same as merchants and officers? For this
reason, Paul's missionary journeys were accompanied
by slave riots. That was the real reason for the first per-
secution of Christians. Religion itself did not matter to
the Romans, but egalitarianism did. The Roman citi-
zen Saul/Paul was, in the end, crucified, upside down,
in his hometown of Rome. In the eyes of the Roman
rulers, this was only a penance for his betrayal."

"And that is where the Vatican is located today," I added softly. "Did Jesus manage to walk alone to Kashmir?" I wanted to know.

"No," Dr. Kashmiri answered. "At least two disciples from Bethany and his mother accompanied him. Apparently, his mother Mary did not endure the hardships. She died on the way. Her grave is located just a few miles west of today's Rawalpindi in Pakistan. Her tomb chapel is called *Mai Mari*—'The resting place of Mother Mary.'"

Oh my goodness! I thought. According to Catholic doctrine, the mother of Jesus ascended into heaven with her physical body. What other surprises were waiting for me?

Dr. Hassnain gave me an understanding look. "Jesus wandered into the local highlands and was warmly received by his tribal brothers. He married, fathered children, and died of old age. He was revered by the common people as well as the political upper class. Come on, Mr. von Däniken, we will visit his grave."

THE JESUS GRAVE

The Jesus grave actually exists. (Because I've covered it in previous books,[4] here are only the most important aspects.) In the middle of Srinagar lies a narrow street with the fitting name of *A Prophet will come.*

On this street is a stone building with three roofs each just above the other. *Rauzabal Khanyar* is the name of the building. In a darkened room within is a cross with candles burning next to it. Behind it is a

FIGURE 2.3: The Jesus Street in Srinagar

shrine with a double-sided, small door. On the floor, enclosed by a wooden frame, is an elevated, rectangular monolith. Under it is where Jesus's sarcophagus is supposedly located. On the wooden plaque in front of the shrine is the inscription *Ziarat Yousa*, the Tomb of Jesus. Inside the shrine is a second inscription: "Here lies Yusa, the famous prophet of the children of Israel."

FIGURE 2.4: Doors of the shrine opened to the grave

FIGURE 2.5: Wooden decoration above the grave, covered with flowers and a flag

FIGURE 2.6: The 2000-year-old grave of Jesus

THE INVENTED ORIGINAL TEXTS

I visited the grave in the fall of 1974. Two years later, my late friend Andreas Faber-Kaiser published his book *Jesus lebte und starb in Kaschmir (Jesus Lived and Died in Kashmir)*, which contained all available documents, so they are accessible to anyone who wants to know more.[5]

For Christian-educated people, the revelations about a grave of Jesus in Kashmir can be devastating. I felt this way at the time. Over the years, I have learned that the New Testament is not what the faithful think it is. The evangelists were not eyewitnesses to the life of Jesus. Only after the destruction of Jerusalem by the Roman Emperor Titus in the year 70 AD did they begin to write about Jesus. Since Jesus, according to the biblical view, ascended into heaven in the year 33 AD, at the earliest, forty years later, the evangelist Mark wrote down his "good news." Dr. Johannes Lehmann, cotranslator of a modern Bible, remarks: "The evangelists are interpreters, not biographers . . . They did not write down history but created history."[6] The Christian believer thinks the gospels were based on so-called original texts, but those do not actually exist. What do you hold in your hands? Without exception, copies of transcripts that originated between the fourth and the tenth century. Of these 1500 copies, not one is consistent with another. Over 80,000 (!) deviations were counted. Not one page of these original texts is without contradictions. The most prominent of these texts is the *Codex Sinaiticus*—created, like the *Codex Vaticanus,* during the fourth century AD—which was found in 1844 in the Sinai Monastery. It contains no less than 16,000 corrections.[7] Friedrich Delitzsch, author of a Hebrew dictionary and a first-class expert, found 3,000 transcription errors in this original text alone.[8]

The theory of original texts is a misleading postulation, and every learned theologian knows this. Normal ordinary men and women associate the term *original text* with something like a document, something like a doubtless first draft; in any case, they think of it as an undisputed and indisputable document. I am always amazed at how the fairytale of the Word of God has lasted for millennia. The fact that these original texts, which are full of contradictions and falsifications, are still sold as the Word of God borders on schizophrenia.

Meanwhile, as an eighty-year-old researcher in the vineyard of the Lord, I have learned how the Christian man works. He does not want to know that his religion is not right, nor does he care about a Jesus grave in the highlands of India. He wants to keep his inner peace. He *wants* to be lied to.

OLD INDIAN VEDAS

After a few days of talks and sightseeing in the highlands of India, I flew to Calcutta. My publisher Aijt Dutt had invited me. After I held a lecture at the university, I met Professor Dileep Kumar Kanjilal for the first time. It was the beginning of a long friendship and extensive correspondence that continues today.[9]

Dr. Kanjilal was born on August 1, 1933, in Calcutta. He studied Sanskrit at the University of Calcutta, did his doctoral thesis on *A Reconstruction of the Text of Sakuntala,* was a visiting professor at various universities, among them Oxford, and is the author of countless scientific articles and several books on special texts from Sanskrit literature. At our first meeting in the Sanskrit College of Calcutta, he, scholarly but with a short stature, commented mockingly on my interest: "You know nothing about Sanskrit! You can study it for forty years, and even then you have just read a fraction of the existing literature."

How should I respond to that? The man was right. But first, I wanted to know exactly how old the Vedic texts actually are.

FIGURE 2.7: Dr. Kanjilal in conversation with Erich von Däniken

"The original religious traditions were most likely created around 5000 BC, although Western scholars doubt it. They were copied again and again, much like the old bibles in your culture."

"In my lecture at the university yesterday, I quoted some passages from the ancient Indian epic *Mahabharata*. There is talk of flying vehicles. Were at least my quotes correct?"

Dr. Kanjilal laughed out loud. "They were correct, but they're absolutely incomplete. If you do not point out the many links at a university talk, you will not be taken seriously by the professionals."

That really shocked me. I learned that thousands of Sanskrit texts were stored in monasteries and even Indian scholars do not have a complete overview of them.

"The ancient Indian Vedas—*veda*, by the way, means knowledge—are the oldest literature of the people of India, perhaps even in the world. These Vedas are, so to speak, a collection of all scriptures that are considered of supernatural origin and inspired by it. In total, there are four large blocks of these Vedas. The 1028 hymns of the *Rigveda* are addressed to the individual gods. They are complemented by the old Indian national epic *Mahabharata* with approximately 160,000 verses. Then there is the *Ramayana* with another 24,000 stanzas—a type of lyrical meter consisting of two quatrains. And finally, the *Puranas*. Here is a list of the *Puranas*; then you will know how little you Europeans know about our literature."

Dr. Kanjilal gave me a note whose contents I give here.

- *Visnu Purana,* 23,000 verses
- *Naradiya Purana,* 25,000 verses
- *Padma Purana,* 55,000 verses
- *Garuda Purana,* 19,000 verses
- *Varaha Purana,* 18,000 verses
- *Bhagavata Purana,* 18, 200 verses
- *Brahmanda Purana,* 12,000 verses
- *Brahmavaivarta Purana,* 18,000 verses
- *Markandeya Purana,* 9,000 verses
- *Bhavisya Purana,* 14,500 verses
- *Vamana Purana,* 10,000 verses
- *Brahma Purana,* 10,000 verses
- *Matsya Purana,* 14,000 verses
- *Kurma Purana,* 17,000 verses
- *Linga Purana,* 10,000 verses
- *Siva Purana,* 24,000 verses
- *Skanda Purana,* 81,000 verses
- *Agni Purana,* 1,400 verses

Against this river of information, our Bible actually becomes a trickle. Dr. Kanjilal dictated to me ancient texts that were teeming with flying vehicles, space habitats, and terrible weapons. Each sentence is exactly quoted with the relevant text passage. I published a lengthy copy from Dr. Kanjilal's extensive knowledge in my book *Habe ich mich geirrt? (Was I Wrong?)*[10] The following short excerpt proves how enlightening and verifiable his research is.

The flying vehicles are called "Rathas" in the Rigveda.[11] The word is translatable as "vehicle" or "car." The Rbhus constructed a flying wagon for the Asvinas twins. With this flying wagon, you could fly everywhere, even beyond the top cloud layers and into "heaven." The hymns mention that the speed of the flying wagon was faster than that of any thought. The aircraft was said to be large, consisting of three parts and triangular. The vehicle had three wheels, which were pulled in during flight.[12]

I was also interested in why the ancient Indian texts were only now being examined for information on flying machines.

Here is Dr. Kanjilal's response:

The translators of the nineteenth and twentieth century were clouded by their zeitgeist, the spirit of their time. For example, the Ramayana talk about a flying wagon that makes the mountains tremble, rises with thunder, burns forests, meadows, and the tops of buildings. Professor Albert Ludwig then commented on the text: "There is no doubt that this can only describe a tropical storm"[13] Or take's translation from 1893. He simply omits entire passages that seemed superfluous to him. He amended passages with parenthetical remarks like "senseless chatter" or "this passage can be safely omitted, it only contains fantasy."[14] At that time another zeitgeist prevailed, Mr. von Däniken. The scholars were all clever and honest, but at the same time, blind and inoculated by the Bible. You could not imagine space-crafts or flying palaces. Today we know better.

(Dr. Kanjilal's pioneering work is available in English.[15] It is a treasure trove for anyone who wants to find out about the flying machines and spaceships in antiquity.)

There was something else I really wanted to ask during that first conversation with Dr. Kanjilal. After all, I was sitting across from the expert, who was probably the only one who could provide the information I wanted:

"Could these flying vehicles, which are also mentioned in the Bible with the prophet Ezekiel and in the *Book of the Kings* of the Ethiopians, not have easily been built on Earth? Or do these really require extraterrestrials?"

Dr. Kanjilal replied, "Throughout Sanskrit literature, there is no line indicating technicians, factories, or test flights. The heavenly vehicles were just suddenly there. Gods created and piloted them. Innovation, planning, and execution did not take place on our planet. There was no evolution. Nothing that would have been developed step by step. And if, in individual cases, people worked on flying vehicles, then they were just the journeymen, the assistants, so to speak, to some master technicians."

Well, I thought, if the development of flying machines had taken place on Earth, Mars would have been a colony of Earth long ago.

CHAPTER 3

Egyptian Connections

I n which you will learn about the following:

*My First Visit to Egypt • An Inexplicable
Experience • Tombs for Monsters • The Sealed
Sarcophagus • Where Did They Vanish To? •
Murders in the Land on the Nile • Visit with
Holeil Ghaly • Rudolf Gantenbrink and I •
Upuaut and the Official Lies • New Riddles
About the Pyramids*

MY FIRST VISIT TO EGYPT

I was just nineteen years old when I first sat on a camel
in front of the big pyramids. How does a nineteen-year-
old Swiss lad come to Egypt?

The Jesuit boarding school—the Collège Saint-
Michel in Friborg, Switzerland—that I attended for five

years not only admitted Catholics, but also members of other faiths. The student who sat next to me in class, Michel Grand, was a Coptic Christian. He was raised in the country on the Nile; his father was Egyptian, his mother French. Michel wore the frizzy, black hairstyle that was common in Arab countries, but his face and complexion were more European looking. During the summer break of 1954, I had planned to join the Swiss military cadet school, but Michel had invited me to Egypt, which was more important. I caught up with the RS (*Rekrutenschule*), the military cadet school, a few months later.

Michel and I began our journey by taking the train to Marseilles, where we boarded a French passenger ship, the *Maréchal Joffre,* for a few days. The ship was

FIGURE 3.1: *Nineteen-year-old student Erich von Däniken on a camel in front of the pyramids*

"Rauzabal Khanyar" is the name of the building with the tomb of Jesus.

A wooden shrine; in it, the Jesus grave

The inscription reads, *Ziarat Yousa,* the Tomb of Jesus.

The sliding door cut out of the alabaster block

Remains of a flower arrangement, several thousand years old

Inside the tomb of Unas in Saqqara

Rudolf Gantenbrink searched for openings on the top of the pyramid.

Old photograph of the Band of Holes from *National Geographic* (color added)

Close-up shot of the Band of
Holes in the Pisco Valley, Peru

Close-up shot of the Band of
Holes in the Pisco Valley, Peru

Descending to the "Lost City" in the Columbian jungle

Padre Carlos Crespi in Cuenca, Ecuador

Five-hundred-kilogram steel springs
secure the area of Space Command.

Inside Space Command

old, and I learned that Maréchal Joffre had been a famous French marshal in the First World War.

When we arrived in Alexandria, we were greeted by a servant who referred to Michel as Monsieur Grands. The Grands didn't only have a "grand" name, they were also well off. After leaving the city, the car drove on a paved road partly through the desert, and partly through magnificent green landscapes at the Nile delta up to Cairo, past the pyramids. In spite of my longing looks, we did not stop anywhere.

The family lived on a large estate with gardens that surrounded a one-story manor house. A wall almost three meters high enclosed the estate. Perplexed, I registered the stark difference between the land on both sides of the wall—within the wall, artificial irrigation provided colorful vegetation; outside the wall, there was only desert with a few scattered bushes. We had arrived on the *Maréchal Joffre* that morning, but by the time we arrived at Michel's the midday heat was beating down on Cairo. After a short meal, my friend Michel suggested we take a nap, which was a common practice. The same servant assigned me a room.

How was I going to be able to sleep? I wondered. For the first time, I was in Egypt, in the fascinating country of which I had learned some secrets from books. I was not even remotely tired. I couldn't be still. I walked softly over polished stone floors that strongly smelled of floor wax, and into the garden beyond. And thus started my first adventure.

AN INEXPLICABLE EXPERIENCE

About twenty meters from the terrace entrance, I was amazed to see flowers and leaves that I had never seen before. But suddenly, the barking of dogs penetrated the silence, and behind me, two splendid Dobermans burst out of the bushes. With lowered heads and wide-open eyes, they growled at me, their bodies ready to leap. These black monsters blocked my way back to the porch. At that time in my life, I was afraid of dogs. Only much later, when my wife and I raised large Great Danes in the house, did I lose that fear. But at that moment, it seemed to me that the animals sensed my fear. "Good dogs, lovely dogs," I said stupidly in Swiss-German and moved backward step by step. Then I felt the wall at my back, and as if by the inspiration of a guardian angel I suddenly knew: *there was a small door—a few meters to the right.* I pushed toward it, still reassuringly talking to the animals, and grabbed the two bars on the door. My guardian angel commanded that I reach as high as my waist. On the bottom side of the screen of the door, my fingers felt a recessed piece of metal that I could push up. Carefully, so as not to frighten the dogs, I opened the door and acrobatically forced my body through it. The Dobermans were ready to leap. But at least now between them and me was the screen. The dogs kept barking and would have probably torn me apart at that point if I had still been on the same side of the door. Unfortunately, I had not completely closed the screen door from the outside—the lock hadn't snapped shut.

One of the ferocious guard dogs pushed it open with its snout, and I started to run for my life. I only wore slippers on my feet, and outside the wall was sandy desert. The slippers quickly flew off, and I was unable to run fast in the sand. I hurried along the wall and suddenly I knew, even in this scene out of a bad dream, that *around the corner there was another screen door and that the mechanism to open it was on the top!* I reached the screen door three meters ahead of my pursuers, and quickly depressed the button on the top metal bar. In a blind panic, I tore open the door, darted through, and pulled the screen entirely shut this time. From the outside, the Dobermans clashed against it. They howled and barked as if they were crazy.

I was soaking wet with sweat, breathing heavily, and trying again to calm the watchdogs beyond the door. Then I noticed that a servant stood beside me. He understood the situation immediately, ran back into the house, and came back with two collars.

At dinner, Michel's father asked me in astonishment: "How did you know about the two screen doors? You couldn't possibly have suspected that the secret latches, which, incidentally, are embedded in the metal struts, must be operated differently. For the smaller screens, they are mounted from the inside at about belly height, whereas for the higher screens, they are hidden on the top metal bar. Nobody should be able to come in from the outside."

At home in Switzerland, I was not familiar with iron doors that had secret locks. So how did I know about the metal screens and the hidden mechanisms at different heights in these doors, in a location outside of Cairo, where I had spent just one hour? Even now, it's still a mystery to me. But without the suggestive inspiration that I had received when I was in dire need, the Dobermans would have mangled me.

TOMBS FOR MONSTERS

The next morning, we were chauffeured by a servant right up to the Great Pyramids and were handed off to two Egyptology students who had been hired to guide us.

It is only a few kilometers from the pyramids to Saqqara. Back then, in 1954, the road was gravel. On the left side of the road was a sewage canal, which stank terribly. Before we exited the car to visit the Step Pyramid of Saqqara, we received expert instruction from the students. I was very impressed. They spoke French and seemed to know everything. At 5:00 pm, one of them asked if we had the courage to climb into an underground labyrinth. We responded that we did! At that time, extensive excavation was taking place in Saqqara. You could see workers everywhere with very basic equipment: shovels, spades, buckets, ropes, and donkeys, and interspersed between them—with brushes and scales—were archaeologists, most of whom knelt in holes and took notes.

The archeologists and workers all knew each other. People were shouting, waving, laughing. Lamps,

FIGURE 3.2: *In the camp of the excavators at Saqqara, Egypt*

torches, and candles changed hands. Following our guides, we entered a corridor under the desert that was tall and wide enough to drive in with a tractor. On both sides of the corridor were niches that contained the largest sarcophagi I have ever seen in my life. At this time, I noticed that a young archaeologist had joined our four-man crew. The cone of light from the headlight he wore scurried across a smoothly polished block of stone. Courageously, I asked, "What's in there?"

"Bulls, young man, holy bulls. All of them mummified," was the reply.

A few steps further was a wide niche in the vault, next to the bulls' sarcophagi. The same was true on the other side of the corridor. I could see gigantic monster sarcophagi as far as the light of the headlamp reached. With every step, we whirled up dust. And I kept on seeing new niches, new sarcophagi.

The experience felt very eerie. The fine dust irritated my throat, so I held a handkerchief in front of my nose. I saw that all the bull caskets were open; their granite lids, which I later learned weighed up to 30 tons a piece, rested on the sarcophagi, just pushed to the side a bit. I wanted to see a bull mummy and asked my companions for help getting up high enough to see. Climbing up on their hands, hips, and shoulders, I reached the top edge of a sarcophagus and laid down on my belly.

"The lamp, please!" I called down.

When it was handed up to me, I could see that the interior of the sarcophagus was spotless—and empty. I tried four more sarcophagi with the same result. Where were the bull mummies? Had they been removed? Put in a museum? I asked the archaeologist, but he shrugged.

"Probably taken out when this was discovered in 1851," he said.

Since then, I've visited the Serapeum—that's the official name for the site—several times. I have studied the story of its discovery and now know that there were never actually any bull mummies in the huge containers. The detailed account of this is in my book *Die Augen der Sphinx* (*The Eyes of the Sphinx*).[1]

Thirty-three years after my visit as a young man, I sat across from Dr. Holeil Ghaly. At that time, in the 80s, he was the chief excavator at Saqqara. His official title was Director of Antiquities Administration in Saqqara.

I said to him: "Professor, I have studied the excavation report written by Auguste Mariette, the man who discovered the Serapeum of Saqqara very thoroughly. Do you know that Mariette never found a sacred bull here?"

Dr. Ghaly thought for a moment, and then replied, "Yes, I know that."

Dr. Ghaly is an approachable, open Egyptologist with a phenomenal knowledge of his field. We have met several times and have also discussed things that were not meant for the public. I have always honored such secrecy agreements. Why? Should not a researcher such as myself, on the hunt for the impossible, publish what he finds out?

Well, suppose I had publicized things entrusted to me in secrecy. And then a journalist wants to review

FIGURE 3.3: Dr. Holeil Ghaly, director of the Antiquities Administration in Saqqara

my testimony and asks Dr. Ghaly to confirm it. He must then protect himself and say that Mr. von Däniken must have misunderstood him. Now I am seen as a liar and I have ruined our personal relationship. Moreover, rumors travel at lightning speed in professional circles: Do not confide in Däniken! He abuses your trust! It was, after all, Dr. Ghaly who made the extraordinary visit to the sepulcher of Sekhemkhet possible. I was allowed to write about that visit, but I would rather keep the follow-up story to myself.

Sekhemkhet? you might be wondering. Who is this?

THE SEALED SARCOPHAGUS

In 1951, archaeologist Dr. Zakaria Goneim discovered a wall in the desert sand, southwest of the Step Pyramid of Saqqara.

In the following months of excavation, the outlines of a huge enclosure with the dimensions of 546 by 185 meters became visible. Finally, Dr. Goneim came across two steps of a pyramid with a base length of 120 meters. In January 1954, after more than two years of excavation, they unearthed a rectangular shaft carved out of the rock, leading underground. Dr. Goneim and his crew worked hard with pickaxes and shovels and gradually worked through the layers of rock. At a depth of 32 meters, they found a locked door, which had obviously never been breached by grave robbers, for the seal was untouched. Finally, they got the door open and found themselves in an underground room that

FIGURE 3.4: *A shaft, cut into the rock, leading to the grave of Sekhemkhet*

was 8.9 meters long, 5.2 meters wide, and 4.5 meters high. By studying the inscriptions and potteries, they discovered to whom the grave belonged—Djoserteti, who had ruled under the Horus name Sekhemkhet during the third dynasty. That was around 2700 BC, or about 4700 years ago, if we use the present time as a point of reference. And so Sekhemkhet was older than Cheops of the Great Pyramid.

Sekhemkhet's actual burial room had been carved out of the rock and left that way. It had no polished monoliths, no paintings on the walls. But it did have 21 armlets on the floor, 388 golden beads, 420 faience ornaments, and a gilded staff. At the center of the cave was the magnificent sarcophagus, made of white alabaster, a type of marble. The sarcophagus was entirely carved out of a single alabaster block. On top of it lay the millennia-old remains of a flower arrangement, which someone must have put there as the last tribute to the deceased pharaoh. Dr. Goneim immediately understood what kind of "great find" luck he had been given. On the one hand, the layer of plant remains was proof that the sarcophagus had not been opened; on the other hand, the plant material allowed a precise dating by the C-14 method. (With carbon 14, exact-age determinations are possible as far back as 10,000 BC.) To ensure that the plant material would not be contaminated, either by the excavators' breath or by some other means, or perhaps be blown away by a draft, Dr. Goneim covered it with a rectangular wooden lid.

In the following days, Dr. Goneim had the sarcophagus and the cave examined meticulously. There was no evidence that the grave had been opened in the past 4700 years. There was not even a trace of an attempted use of force to break in.

FIGURE 3.5: *Wooden lid to protect the bouquet*

Sarcophagi usually have heavy lids, but in this case, everything was different. Like an animal cage, the sarcophagus of Sekhemkhet had a sliding door at the front. Carved out of the alabaster were rails and strips. Obviously, the door could be raised upward. In addition, it sealed the sarcophagus so it was airtight. This was a unique and incomparable work of art, the most beautiful and the oldest sarcophagus Egyptologists had ever admired. Never before (and not since) had something like that been discovered in the land on the Nile. Also, the design of this sarcophagus did not fit the time period of 2700 BC. Remember, every technology has its evolution: first, it has to be invented, proscribed, and developed. After all, no stonemason starts hitting the rock at random. A blow in the wrong place and the block would have been destroyed. So, the sarcophagus, including its sliding door and the corresponding slide rails, had to have been planned and calculated before the first chisel strike, by some Bronze Age Michelangelo. In addition, there was an unbroken seal stuck between the sliding door and the sarcophagus's wall. Such skill and workmanship must have been for someone very important. There was no longer any doubt: the mummy of Sekhemkhet rested in the alabaster chest. So Dr. Goneim informed the Egyptian government and, with their permission, some journalists. They should all be witnesses to the sensational burial site.

On June 26, 1954, the time had come. Egyptian government officials and selected archaeologists and journalists from all over the world were invited. Movie cameras and photo cameras had been installed, and the subterranean space was illuminated with spotlights. Even chemicals were ready in case some piece of the mummy had to be protected from immediate decay right on the spot. Everyone stared at the sarcophagus. Indescribable feelings of hope and honor erupted in Dr. Goneim. Then he gave the command to open it.

Two workers pushed knives, then chisels, into the barely visible gap at the bottom of the opening. Thin ropes were kept ready to pull up the sliding door. The show of strength lasted a full two hours. Had a curse been put on this casket, or were the laws of vacuum having a big impact? Finally, a tiny gap appeared at the bottom; the door had moved a few millimeters. Knives got stuck in it, stronger chisels were placed in it, and, using leverage, the workers planned to finally push the damned thing up. There was a groan from the alabaster, as if it was fighting the intrusion. But the first few inches were open. Immediately, workers clamped an iron rail in the gap so the door could not slip back again. Silently, dripping with sweat, and feeling very tense, the representatives of the public observed the fight with the alabaster. Slowly, one small push at a time, the workers opened the door. After every inch gained, they would push wood pegs into the opening. These pegs were still in the sarcophagus thirty-three years later when my friend Rudolf Eckhardt and I photographed it.

When the door was finally open, Dr. Goneim was the first to kneel down, shining his light expectantly into the dark opening. He shined the light in again, and again. And then, puzzled, he stood up. The magnificent alabaster chest turned out to be sparkling clean—and empty. An impossibility! After all, the entrance to the underground crypt was unbroken, no grave robbers had ever entered the room, gold-plated pearls and other valuables were untouched. There were neither tunnels nor any signs of burglars. There was, however, the last flower offering on the sarcophagus. It probably came from his lover, who was allowed to accompany her master down to the crypt. In addition, the totally closed sliding door with the unbroken seal of the pharaoh seemed to confirm expectations. So where was the mummy?

Because I am familiar with many ancient texts, I remembered a passage by the historian Diodorus of Sicily. He lived in Alexandria for a long time in the first century BC. He knew the texts of his ancestors and became the author of a forty-volume history library. In the first book of his work, Diodorus wrote that the gods once lived on Earth. They were the ones who changed mankind's cannibalistic ways. "These gods grew wheat and barley, instructed people in the craft of mining and named many things for which no previous expressions existed."[2]

WHERE DID THEY VANISH TO?

And where are the corpses of these gods? Diodorus knows: "What is told about the burial of these gods is contradictory, mainly because the priests were forbidden to pass on the exact knowledge of these things communicated to them. That's why they were not allowed to tell the people the truth, because of the danger that this covert wisdom about the gods would bring to the masses."

Diodorus had written about the funeral of the gods. And everything about these funerals had to be kept secret. When I stood in this ancient hall of rocks, older than the Cheops Pyramid, the contradictions hit me like the restrained giggling of these gods. The strength and simultaneous delicacy of Sekhemkhet's alabaster sarcophagus did not fit this hole in the rock. Did I stand in front of one of the sleeping pods of one of the legendary gods? Had an offspring of a god slept here? Maybe not for eternity, but only for a few decades or centuries, until his space-traveling colleagues picked him up and resurrected him? Does this sound absurd?

Today there are two palaces of dead people in Florida, where frozen corpses are waiting to be resurrected in the future. We are looking for ways to put astronauts in a deep-sleep-like state on their long journeys. Had time run out for the offspring of the gods? Had he been seriously ill? Was it all about hibernating the body with the right medicine and waiting for the comrades in the mother ship to come back, aim some device at him, and beam him out? This could have made a burial chamber decorated with magnificent monoliths and colored pictures superfluous, and even, perhaps, dangerous! After all, the more artists who worked in a splendor grave, the more gossip they would create. A wonderfully decorated chamber would have meant many would have entered the subterranean space for years, and that would have been exactly what should have been avoided. Once the buried being was in deep sleep, no stonemason, no priest, and no artist should have been allowed to visit this underground space. This was a divine command: because the priests were forbidden from passing on their shared knowledge of these things (Diodorus).

Was the sarcophagus of the alleged Sekhemkhet in reality never breached by any unauthorized persons, but opened and closed again by the only authorized crew? Now they had their sleeping god, and the scientists of the future might wonder how in the world the mummy had escaped from a closed and sealed sarcophagus.

All of these were speculative thoughts that flashed through my mind when I stood in front of the empty alabaster sarcophagus.

—

This time, my visit was only possible because of the friendship I shared with Dr. Holeil Ghaly. I asked him if other similarly empty sarcophagi existed.

Dr. Ghaly replied, "Harvard University archaeologists from the United States discovered the tomb of Hetepheres I in Giza in 1925. She was the wife of Snofru and presumably the mother of Cheops. The sarcophagus was made from alabaster just like Sekhemkhet's, however, without a sliding door. There was a heavy lid on top of the trunk. And as with Sekhemkhet, there wasn't any doubt that no one had ever entered the grave 27 meters below the ground. Everything was untouched: golden armlets, golden plates on the floor, a gold-trimmed carriage—no thief had ever entered the burial chamber. Here, too, the sarcophagus's lid bore an unbroken seal. Then the same riddle as with Sekhemkhet: the inside was sparkling clean and empty. We suspect that these could have been fake graves. However, this is contradicted by the gold and the jewelry in the crypts. Fake tombs are not filled with treasures . . . ."

Fake graves. Why should pharaohs have created fake tombs? It took the same hard work to break them out of the rock as it did real tombs. To mislead the tomb robbers is the classic answer. But—not with

Sekhemkhet! Why not? you ask. The pyramids began with the Step Pyramid of Saqqara (around 2650 BC). Before that, no pharaoh was ever buried. Djoser, the builder of the Step Pyramid of Saqqara, belonged to the same third dynasty as the vanished Sekhemkhet. But at that time, there were no grave robbers. The pharaohs of the third dynasty did not know any broken tombs—that came later. So why should they have had passages and tombs so laboriously driven into the rocks? Why fill fake graves with gold and precious stones when the graves of their ancestors had not been robbed?

Incidentally, the opening in the rock leading to Sekhemkhet's burial chamber has long since been covered again with sand. Access is now impossible.

And disconcertingly, death is now associated with the discovery of this tomb. The discoverer of the underground facility himself, Dr. Goneim, committed suicide in 1959.

MURDERS IN THE LAND ON THE NILE

Others associated with these tombs have also been killed. Here's a terrible example I can relate.

Every few years, I act as a travel guide for members of the Ancient Astronaut Society (AAS) to Egypt. (I will relate more about the AAS later in this book.) Thanks to my relationships in Egypt and enough baksheesh, every time, I am able to lead the Däniken AAS group to inaccessible places. For example, one year, I lead them to the Serapeum with its gigantic sarcophagi, and into the unfinished chamber or pond under the ramp to the pyramid. This is not accessible to "normal" tourists. For decades, my group was accompanied by an Egyptologist I refer to as Adel, who was a very educated and reserved person, and who, I later learned, worked for the Egyptian secret service. I knew Adel so well that he even tried to find an Egyptian publisher for one of my books. I agreed to provide the financing of the translation from German into High Arabic, but we never got the chance, as I will now relate.

At one point frustrated at our lack of progress finding a publisher, I asked Adel, "Why on earth does no Arab publisher want to print my books? We have a completely finished Arabic translation."

Adel replied, "Your books are about 'gods,' and gods are a sacrilege to any Muslim, a mortal sin, so to speak. There is only *one* God: Allah."

"But Adel, we both know that the word *gods* in my books is just a misunderstanding. In fact, there are no gods but Allah. But our technically uneducated Stone Age ancestors believed that the aliens were gods. Can we not explain this difference to Arab publishers and intellectuals? After all, the ancient historians, from Strabo to Plutarch and Herodotus to Diodorus or even the Egyptian Manetho, also speak of gods!"

"You are right, Erich. But this difference cannot be taught to the uneducated people, much less the imams."

As a result, none of my books has ever been published in an Arab country. Faith makes it impossible and the publishers and booksellers are scared to go against such powerful beliefs. However, censorship is powerless against TV series. That's how the History Channel's 175-episode series *Ancient Aliens* manages to flicker across Arab TV screens.

But the tragedy is that my friend Adel was shot dead on November 17, 1997, by Arab terrorists. This happened at the terrorist attack in the forecourt of the funerary temple of Hatshepsut in Deir-el-Bhari on the east side of the Nile in Luxor. On that sad November day, thirty-six Swiss people died, as did ten Japanese, six British, four Germans, two Columbians, and one Egyptian named Adel. He had run toward one of the raging terrorists and had shouted, "Stop it now!" The terrorist shot several bullets directly into the face of his brother-in-faith Adel. In the name of Allah.

ANOTHER VISIT WITH HOLEIL GHALY

At a dinner at the Sheraton Hotel in Cairo, Dr. Holeil Ghaly once asked me: "Do you know the pyramid texts?" At the time, I had read about them but had never seen one of the original texts. The next day, when Dr. Ghaly and I were out in the field, he stopped his jeep in front of a large hole in the ground of Saqqara. "Pepi I," he lectured, "ruled from 2289 to 2255 BC. We shouldn't get in the way right now. A French team is in the process of taking measurements." Shortly afterward we parked in front of the tomb of Unas, a pharaoh of the Fifth Dynasty (2356–2323 BC). Stooped over, we proceeded down a tunnel at an angle. When we reached the actual burial chamber, I saw that even the vestibule was filled with many inscriptions. Then, in the sanctuary, we encountered a black basalt sarcophagus.

The walls and ceilings were literally plastered with hieroglyphic texts.

Such texts were also found in the crypts of Pepi, Seti, and other pharaohs. The experts sort and arrange these texts into so-called *utterances* (numbered sayings). On this particular visit I asked Dr. Ghaly about these:

"What do you make of these?"

"The pharaohs believed in another life after death. In a new world. The pyramid texts express their wishes and ideas."

FIGURE 3.6: Dr. Holeil Ghaly and Erich von Däniken in conversation

"And if not . . . ?"I asked.

"What do you mean . . .?"

I ventured, "Maybe it was not about imaginations of another world but rather about giving thanks for this world . . ."

"I don't follow you anymore!"

Let me make my point clear: In the pyramid texts of Unas, Osiris is equated with the constellation Orion. He drives "to the heavenly road." Osiris is a "horizon dweller" who, with his ship, "pushes off from the Earth" and "ascends to heaven" (Utterance 303).

In addition, Utterance 267 states: "A staircase to heaven has been set up for me, and I rose high on the smoke of the great vessel . . . and thundered across the sky in your barque. I may lift off from the land in your barque."[3] And Utterance 584 states: "The doors of the [?, unreadable] that are in the firmament, were opened to me. The metal doors that are in the starry sky. . . ." Confronted with such statements, someone like me had to think of something other than psychologically interpreted wishes for a life after death.

RUDOLF GANTENBRINK AND I

On March 22, 1993, a sensational event of the first order occurred in the Great Pyramid. German robotic designer and builder Rudolf Gantenbrink placed a small robot named Upuaut in an airshaft at the southern side of the Queen's chamber; from there, it drove through the shaft at an upward angle. After more than

60 meters, the robot came to a stop in front of a small door with two copper fittings. The surprise of finding this door was complete, because up to this point, Egyptologists had only spoken of an airshaft or a symbolic shaft. Despite this phenomenal discovery, at first the press did not hear anything about it. The discovery was kept secret—even by me. I knew about this because of my personal connection Rudolf Gantenbrink, and I had promised him to keep it secret. But how did our first meeting come about?

In February 1993, I once again stayed in Saqqara and spent time visiting tombs and ruins. Afterward, I headed for the bar at Hotel Mövenpick in Giza. I was tired, thirsty, and unshaven. The person sitting across from me looked at least as scruffy as I did. We stared at each other for some time, until the stranger said in German:

"Somehow, you look like this Däniken guy . . ."

"The original," I nodded in reply. "What brings you to Egypt?" I asked.

"You're the last person I'd confide in," the stranger said and then he laughed in a friendly way.

He seemed to be carrying a secret and thought I was an esoteric—one of these "pyramidiots" to whom you should not confide any truths.

In the end, I learned his name, which didn't mean anything to me at the time, and after an objective talk and some wine, we began to respect each other. Later on, he began calling me by my first name and said: "If you promise not to tell anyone what I'm doing here, especially not a journalist, I can confide in you."

The rest is history. Ever since that night, Rudolf Gantenbrink and I have been friends. That evening, at the Hotel Mövenpick in Giza, we eventually went to his room where he demonstrated how the robot Upuaut worked. Like little boys, we squatted on the floor and played with Upuaut. Rudolf also showed me the most amazing video sequences that Upuaut had recorded inside the shaft.

If you are interested in learning more about the Upuaut robot, visit the Jungfraupark in Interlaken, Switzerland, where it currently resides.

UPUAUT AND THE OFFICIAL LIES

How did Rudolf Gantenbrink ever come up with the far-fetched idea of the robot? After all, he did not belong

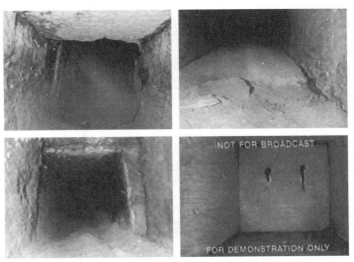

FIGURE 3.7: *Details from the south shaft inside the pyramid*

to the select circle of Egyptologists. Rudolf explained it to me when I met up with him later in Cairo:

"The whole thing started when I was in Egypt during the Gulf War. I had suggested to Dr. Rainer Stadelmann from the DAI [the German Archaeological Institute in Cairo] that he take a closer look at these airshafts—at that time they were still called airshafts. Shortly thereafter, we began developing a technology that made such things possible. In 1992, we built a ventilation system into the pyramid, which is when we noticed that the old manholes lead to the outside somewhere. That was the starting point of the whole investigation. We called the next project *Upuaut-2,* and of course that name needs some explanation. Dr. Stadelmann explained that Upuaut was an ancient Egyptian god and the word translates as the 'opener of the ways.'"

Which shafts was Dr. Stadelmann referring to? The Great Pyramid contains three chambers, and according to Dr. Stadelmann, this is true of all Egyptian pyramids. Dr. Stadelmann is regarded as the inventor of a three-chamber theory. Any tourist who, sweating profusely, climbs into the Cheops pyramid, will see two chambers. The upper one is generously called the King's Chamber, though no mummy has ever been found in it, and the lower, somewhat smaller chamber, is, accordingly, called the Queen's Chamber. Thirty-five meters vertically under the pyramid is a third chamber, which is unfinished in the case of the Great Pyramid. From both the King's and Queen's chambers, shafts lead into the pyramid rock. At various times, these have been called *airshafts, shafts of souls,* or *symbolic shafts.* The sensational discovery made by Rudolf Gantenbrink robot was in the southern shaft, which leads from the Queen's Chamber into the side wall.

Designating this hole (and other such holes) as an airshaft was nonsense from the outset because the shaft was not opened until 1872, and before that, there had been no hole in the wall. Basically, before 1872, no air could have flowed into the chamber.

How was this particular shaft discovered? In 1872, a British man named Waynman Dixon, hoping to find secret treasures hidden in the pyramid, tapped each centimeter of the walls of the Queen's Chamber with a small hammer. He found two places that sounded hollow. Dixon proceeded to use a pickax to break open the walls in these spots, and by doing so, he discovered the north and south shafts.

Both shafts must have been part of the pyramid's design before construction began. They could not have been chiseled out afterward—they are just too narrow, with side lengths of almost 20 centimeters. Even a child would not fit through them. This is where the Upuaut robot came into the picture.

We owe the idea for this vehicle—its construction, and its actual exploration of the inside of the pyramid— to Rudolf Gantenbrink. He received financial help from the following sponsors: Escape in Geneva, Switzerland (makers of special motors), Hilti in Vaduz, Lichtenstein (specialists in drilling technology), Gore in Munich, Germany (producers of special cable), and Mäurer and Wirtz in Stollberg, Germany.

FIGURE 3.8: *The Upuaut robot*

One would think Gantenbrink's dedication and personal achievements in this field would be appreciated by Egyptologists. Nowadays, when an astronomer discovers a new star or comet, the celestial body often receives the name of the discoverer. But such recognition was not to be in Gantenbrink's case. Although Upuaut made its sensational discovery at exactly 11:05 am on March 22, 1993, and both experts in Cairo and those from DAI were very aware of it, an icy silence followed. No message went public. Nobody was allowed to announce anything. Rudolf Gantenbrink showed some of the video that the Upuaut robot had taken during its exploration to some experts, but not to the press. But somehow, a journalist learned about it. Two weeks after the discovery in the pyramid, a small message appeared in the British *Daily Telegraph* entitled "Portcullis Blocks Robot in Pyramid."[4] The message also reached Cairo. And that was when the lies started.

The DAI in Cairo categorically denied the whole thing. "That's complete nonsense!" said the spokeswoman for the organization, Christel Egorov, to news agency *Reuters*.[5] She went further to say that the tunnels discovered were only manholes, and a mini-robot was simply being used to measure the humidity, and that everyone knows that the Great Pyramid contains no more chambers.

These statements were wrong and the DAI knew it. After all, they had already been working for a whole year with Rudolf Gantenbrink at this time. But the untruths got even better: Dr. Rainer Stadelmann, the dean of German Egyptology and director of DAI, flatly denied the possibility of a secret chamber behind the door in the shaft. He explained to journalists: "It is common knowledge that every treasure in the pyramid has long been blundered."[6] His colleague, Egyptologist Dr. Günter Dreyer, confirmed this: "There's nothing behind this door. It's all imagination."[7]

It soon became clear to Rudolf Gantenbrink that the Egyptologists wanted to get rid of him. What had he done wrong? he wondered. Had he been impolite? Unprofessional? Had he come up with unscientific ideas? None of that. Gantenbrink didn't even speculate about the shaft and the door, so why did they want to get rid of him?

He finally spoke to the press, not because he ran to journalists—it was the other way around. Tipped off by British scientists, journalists got wind of the Upuaut exploration and soon after, they closed in on

Gantenbrink. Naturally, he could not lie and claim he had never designed a robot, and so they kept at him.

At this point, the relationship between Rudolf Gantenbrink and Dr. Stadelmann has been severed as had the one between him and the Director of Antiquities Administration in Cairo at the time, Dr. Zahi Hawass.

NEW RIDDLES ABOUT THE PYRAMIDS

What has happened since then? Have discoveries continued?

In September 2002, the National Geographic Society placed a new robot in the Gantenbrink shaft. It was equipped with a small drill. The robot drilled a hole through the door and pushed a tiny camera through. About 18 centimeters behind the first door was a wall.[8] Mark Lehner, the most famous Egyptologist in America, said it was a "symbolic closure" through which the Pharaoh's soul had to travel in order to enter the world of the dead.[9] Dr. Hawass interpreted the wall as "another sealed door." Even the copper fittings on the door couldn't have any practical significance in the eyes of the experts. It was about "symbolic fittings," they said.

The National Geographic Society's robot also passed through the hitherto unknown shaft on the north side of the Queen's Chamber. This shaft does not go up at an angle like the south shaft; it goes around the Great Gallery, which must have complicated the engineer's planning at (supposedly) Cheops's time. This shaft also had a door with two copper fittings, at the same height as the south shaft, that blocked further progress.

After this discovery, years passed. A new robot, dubbed Djedi, passed through the Gantenbrink shaft on the south side. In Arabic, the word *Djedi* means Cheops. This robot drilled a hole that was just big enough to pass an endoscope through into the wall. On the other side, the endoscope showed a small, polished room. At the top of the left wall, something like a red smear or a sign became visible.

Hieroglyphs were widely used in Cheops's time, but whatever this smear was, it was not hieroglyphs.[10]

The experts recognize pure symbolism in everything. Whether it is shafts, fittings, or doors. The soul of the pharaoh is supposed to divide itself, and at the same time, escape through the north and south shafts. Obviously, the poor pharaonic soul has not managed this schizophrenic act of division. Both doors have remained sealed since the construction of the pyramid. May the symbolism-clouded minds of Egyptologists break free someday.

CHAPTER 4

Lied to, Cheated, Abused

In which you will learn about the following:

Swiss Pilot in Brazil • ARD Correspondent Karl Brugger • Tatunca's Exciting Report • Audio Records • An Invisible-Making Belt? • Murder Churning • Tatunca's Exposure • Connection to Ecuador? • Padre Le Paige and the Tombs of Aliens • The Discovery of the Band of Holes • Bribed with a Tobacco Pipe • Heli-Flight into the Unknown • The Treasures of Carlos Crespi

SWISS PILOT IN BRAZIL

On November 18, 1975, I received a sixteen-page, hand-written letter from Manaus, Brazil. The sender was Ferdinand Schmid, unknown to me. He introduced himself as Swiss. He said he was a former Swissair pilot, had been captain of a DC-8, and currently lived in Brazil. From time to time he performed medical flights for *Fundação Nacional do Índio* (FUNAI), the official Indian Conservation Authority of Brazil, with small propeller aircraft. The rest of his letter fascinated me immensely. Ferdinand Schmid said he knew a white Indian person quite well who lived in the upper Amazon and was the chief of a tribe. The guy called himself Tatunca Nara and claimed that in his tribal area, there were underground halls with the technical equipment of an alien civilization left behind millennia ago.

Wow! If that was true . . . ? First, I asked Swissair's human resources department in Zurich if they had a flight captain named Ferdinand Schmid. They confirmed they used to. Mr. Schmid had retired. I then wrote to FUNAI in Manaus and asked for information about this Suizo (Swiss) named Ferdinand Schmid. Like Swissair, the regional director of FUNAI, a Mr. Kazuto Kawamoto, confirmed Schmid's statements. It was only after this confirmatory information about Mr. Schmid that I replied to Manaus and signaled my interest. After the first letter between Ferdinand Schmid and me, I collected a pile of correspondence.[1] Bit by bit, I learned a fantastic story that actually seemed too impossible to be true. Then Ferdinand Schmid visited me in Switzerland. He came across as an educated, thoroughly honest person who was convinced of his story. I was hooked.

ARD CORRESPONDENT
KARL BRUGGER

From Ferdi, as I soon called him, I learned that this Chief Tatunca Nara had light skin because his mother had been a German missionary on the Amazon. Karl Brugger, a German correspondent for ARD Television in Brazil, could attest to this. In the fall of 1976, Karl Brugger published a nonfiction book: *Die Chronik von Akakor (The Chronicle of Akakor)*.[2] Prior to this point, Brugger had been a well-studied historian who had lived in Brazil for many years. In 1974, he became the official correspondent for German radio and the ARD broadcasting station. In Brugger's book everything I learned from Ferdi Schmid was confirmed.

FIGURE 4.1: Ferdinand Schmid and Erich von Däniken

TATUNCA'S EXCITING REPORT

Brugger described how he had met Tatunca Nara and had checked his statements as much as was possible on the Amazon River. According to Tatunca, at around 13,000 BC, spaceships appeared in the sky. When the strangers arrived, they behaved as if they were teachers to all of humanity, but they preferred a chosen people, the tribe of the Ugha Mongulala. The capital of this tribe is said to have been Akakor, a city on the upper Amazon River. At some point after the strangers' first arrival, a terrible flood swept over the earth. Only a few tribes survived. Here is a passage from Brugger's book that covers what happened next:

> Twilight still lay on the face of the earth. Covered were the sun and the moon. There appeared ships in the sky, huge and of golden color. Great was the joy of the surviving servants. Their former masters had returned. And the chosen people brought their gifts. Feathers of the big forest bird, honey from bees, and fruits. Everyone, down to the most common man, looked up at the old fathers. But there weren't many left . . . So only the memories remain for my people, and the rolls and green stones. They are located in the subterranean districts, where, in addition, Lhasa's flying disk and the strange vehicle are located, which can move over mountains and water. This disk has a shiny, golden color and is made of unknown material. It has the shape of a clay roll, tall as two men standing over each other and just as wide. The disk can accommodate two people. It has neither sails nor

oars. But our priest says that Lhasa can fly faster than the fastest eagle and move in the clouds like a leaf in the wind. The strange vehicle is similarly mysterious. Seven long legs carry a large, silver shell. Three of the legs are facing forward, four facing backward. They are similar to curved bamboo rods and are very flexible. At the ends there are rolls the size of a water lily . . ."[3]

For someone like me, who has been following the footprints of the gods since youth, Karl Brugger's book was like an enlightenment. Finally, there seemed to be examples of foreign technologies somewhere on the earth. Ready to be touched. Ready to be photographed. I had to go there, no matter what the cost.

I often talked to Karl Brugger before he died. He has been dead for many years—he was assassinated on January 1, 1984. Brugger was just 41 years old. The perpetrator, who was never found, shot him several times and fled without stealing anything.

My friend Wolfgang Siebenhaar has thoroughly investigated the drama surrounding Karl Brugger and Tatunca Nara. He has even asked questions about Brugger's murder: Who could have possibly been bothered so much by the ARD correspondent? Did the killer use his last chance to get Brugger at the end of his stay in South America because it seemed easier to kill Brugger in Rio de Janeiro than in far-away Germany? (Brugger had intended to travel back to Germany.) Did Brugger's long-term research in terms of Akakor and Tatunca Nara seal his fate?[4]

Karl Brugger was not the only person murdered who was involved in this thriller about Tatunca Nara. Other murders followed. (More about this later).

I began to consider an expedition to this mysterious city of Akakor. I corresponded extensively with Ferdinand Schmid about this possibility, but also with FUNAI in Manaus and some professors in the US.

AUDIO RECORDS

On January 11, 1977, Ferdinand Schmid met with Tatunca Nara in Manaus. Ferdi was supposed to find out whether an expedition team would be welcome in Akakor. With the consent of Tatunca Nara, Ferdinand Schmid taped the conversation. Below is an excerpt from the interview:

FS (Ferdinand Schmid): *Tatunca is with me now. And we will talk about the matter to the extent that this is possible. Today is January 11, 1977.*

Mr. Tatunca, what is the difference between Akakor and Akahim, and why should the planned trip to Akahim be undertaken?

TN (Tatunca Nara): *I, Tatunca Nara, the prince of Akakor, greet and honor the one who has the courage to follow the footprints of the ancestors. I do not know if you're traveling around the world as an idealist or for what reason you seek evidence that the gods were astronauts ... "Aka" means fortification, "kor" means number two, "him" is the number three, and "nis," by the* *way, would mean one. Akanis may have been present in the Old Chronicle, but has never been mentioned in our history. Akakor, the second fortification, harbored the dwellings of our gods or, today, of the living dead, as we call them. Well, Akahim is the third fortification . . . , maybe not as large in size as Akakor. Akahim is stuck to a mountain rock, somehow like Machu Picchu in Peru. The city has underground access . . . Akahim is more of a kind of shipyard, a workshop. There are still a lot of machines, there are lights, there are other machines around, but the technology is alien, not interpretable . . .*

FS: *May I again ask you, Tatunca, to make your statement as to the responsibility that Mr. von Däniken would have to assume?*

TN: *Well, Mr. von Däniken needs to be clear about what would happen after his visit. What will happen after Mr. von Däniken leaves Akahim? If he filmed and took some things? There are consequences of this expedition. Is Mr. von Däniken really clear about what will happen after he has proved that the gods were astronauts? If he shows a technology that has never been in your realm of possibilities? Will civilization be responsible? We do not ask for much. We demand the security for the life and survival of our people. And land for agriculture and livestock. For this we can hand over everything, including the machines of our gods. And how does Mr. von Däniken intend to act toward the great powers? The Russians? The Americans? . . . I do not want my name mentioned in the world public, I want security for my people . . .*

FS: *Well, we can deal with these problems later. Now something else, Tatunca. How do you think you can explain to your people Mr. von Däniken's expedition? And that the participants of this expedition are guaranteed a peaceful stay?*

TN: *As I already said, it is not Mr. von Däniken's expedition that scares us. It's the consequences of that . . . And that's something Mr. von Däniken must think of and for which he has to come up with something. Not only does he have to assert his personal influence, but he has to consult scientists that something will really be done for our safety. Let me tell you frankly: I use the sledgehammer on the machines, for I am staying there in Akahim, am using the sledgehammer against these machines to recall the gods from the universe . . .*

FS: *Well, Tatunca, I think we've discussed various things we can tell Mr. von Däniken. And now I have a list in my hands, the list of requirements for the trip . . .*

TN: *I refuse to be paid. Mr. Schmid, may I briefly interrupt you? I do not ask for it, I do not need money. I do not care about diamonds or gold . . . I've spent five years of my life making contact with civilization and FUNAI and the military. I did not succeed. I always met with contradiction and unbelief. I only require the equipment so that I can quickly go to my people. Then I'll come back in May and get Mr. von Däniken. May he be happy with it in civilization. Däniken is probably the only one who can understand the whole context. The others do not understand . . .*

FS: *Good, then you actually expect Mr. von Däniken only to pay the relevant expenses . . .*

TN: *Yes. But it is necessary that he is here by the end of this month. We are dependent on the rainy season. Otherwise I cannot go home and come back. The distances . . .*

FS: *Well, Mr. Tatunca, it's all about carrying out the expedition now. I will talk about all the issues with Mr. von Däniken. And one more thing that interests Mr. von Däniken very much: When and how were you appointed Chief of the Mongulala?*

TN: *When and how? It was 1970. In 1968 I came back from Germany to Brazil . . .*

FS: *Yes, that too is a question: When and under what circumstances did you come to Germany? What did you do there, and how long was your stay there?*

TN: *Well, I have to go back to 1955 then. My mother died in 1955, and in 1956, we traveled to Akahim. In 1957 we returned. In 1958, my brother-in-law returned to his people in Akahim. In 1959, a Brazilian Air Force plane crashed from the sky. Six officers were captured by our people. My father wanted to kill them. But I knew a great deal about civilization from my mother's explanations. I wanted to get to know these tribes of civilization. And so I left Akakor with the six officers at the end of 1959. They took me to Manaus, and there I was to get some type of document. The registry asked me for my name. I said Tatunca. Then they wanted to know my last name, and I said, "de-u-ascha-nara," which means I do not have a surname. The man who wrote just heard "Nara," and so I got a Brazilian passport in the name of Tatunca Nara. The passport also identified me as* an indigenous person. I was able to move freely with this document. In the harbor was also a German ship. You know that even ocean liners can travel up the broad Amazon to Manaus. Now, for the first time, I heard words and phrases from my mother's people. So the sailors helped me and hid me on board.

In Germany, the Seepolizei (marine police) handed me to all sorts of consulates in Hamburg. I was asked: What nationality does the man have? Since I could not speak Portuguese or Spanish at the time, they said that he speaks German better than anything else. And so I received a German ID "without nationality." In Hamburg, I was taken to a German missionary who had worked in the Amazon rainforest for 30 years. He watched me for some time and said the guy's biggest fear is cars. He should therefore learn to become an auto mechanic . . . But I only did that for a short time and then again worked on a ship. At the end of 1960, I was back in Brazil. FUNAI said I should go home and civilize my tribe. The FUNAI brought me up the Amazon to the Rio Negro and I debarked at Kashmera de Alianza. They made many promises to me, but never kept them and never paid anything. Because they were actually supposed to help our tribe with the task of civilizing it and with goods.

FS: Is Mr. von Däniken the first from civilization who is allowed to visit Akahim?

TN: The Bishop of Acre, Bishop Don Qunde [?, incomprehensible], was the only white man there. He also saw the machines and he took a belt with him. The

*word belt may be wrong, because you can strap it on
and make yourself invisible. The high priest gave it to
the bishop with the promise that he would have to bring
it back in half a year. But after a party in Fejo[?], the
plane crashed. More than 30 people died. We searched
for the belt and still do not know where it is. Our priests
do not know either. The Bishop of Manaus, whom I
also interviewed, said that Don [?] sent many things to
Rome before his death . . .*

FS: *I think Mr. von Däniken has a lot of information
here. I will now take this tape quickly to Switzerland.
Then we can make further plans.*

TN: *I do all this for only two reasons. To finally show
civilization who the original gods were and to ensure
my people's survival. I will even show Mr. von Däniken the living dead, and then he will ask at first: What
now? What now? He cannot load the city of Akahim
piece by piece into his helicopter. He cannot continue
to do that. There are no trucks or roads. He cannot take
anything except small things. So how does he want to
prove it . . . ?"*

AN INVISIBLE-MAKING BELT?

Why did I quote several pages of this conversation? It is
a historic document and proves how cleverly Tatunca
Nara operated. Nothing he said was completely unrea-
sonable. It made sense. But should I not have laughed
out loud and thrown my arms in the air when he was
talking about a belt that made you invisible?

No, because the Greek philosopher Plato in his dialogue *The State* talks about such an object. Here's the abbreviated story:

> *One day a huge storm broke out and earthquakes shook the ground. Gyges, the shepherd, stared into a hole in the ground that had opened up. "Besides several other wonderful objects, he saw some kind of horse, made of iron with windows. Gyges looked in and saw in it also a corpse, larger than that of a normal human. He wore a metal ring that Gyges pulled off him and then climbed back up to the surface of the earth ..."[5] The strange ring was movable and Gyges turned it. As he approached the other shepherds, he suddenly realized they did not see him. Depending on which position Gyges turned the mysterious ring, he became visible or invisible. But even in his invisible state, Gyges heard and saw everything that was going on around him.*

The same Gyges, the former shepherd, later became ruler of the kingdom of Lydia.

The invisible belt of which Tatunca spoke did not mean the end of my thinking process here. Precisely because of my knowledge of the ancient scriptures, I consider many things to be possible that seem impossible to others.

Now I had to organize an expedition to Akahim, somewhere on the upper Amazon. The correspondence with Ferdinand Schmid intensified—the money transfers as well. On July 15, 1977, I met Tatunca Nara for the first time. Our secretary, Willi Dünnenberger, Ferdinand Schmid, and the science fiction author

Walter Ernsting also took part in our meeting. Walter was known by his pseudonym Clark Darlton.

Meanwhile, Ferdinand Schmid was trying to organize an expedition using helicopters. This was all easily said, but was much harder to carry out. Helicopters have only a very limited range. Our helicopters were partially funded by my Brazilian publisher *Melhoramentos* in São Paulo. The flight time to Akahim from Manaus had been calculated to take four hours. One way. Thus, fuel depots would have to be set up on the Amazon and then again on the Rio Negro. In addition, the oil company that rented the helicopters to us demanded we use at least two machines, in case a technical breakdown should occur.

When Ferdinand Schmid finished organizing this he shared the plan with Tatunca Nara. Tatunca had even

FIGURE 4.2: Tatunca Nara and Erich von Däniken

promised to bring a small technical item from Akahim to me. This should be the final valid proof of that story about alien technology. Tatunca never made good on this promise. Even worse, at our meeting on July 15, he suddenly banned the expedition by helicopter, even though everything was already organized and partially paid for in advance by our side. The tape recording with the talks from July 15 has been published by the reliable Wolfgang Siebenhaar in his book *Die Wahrheit über die Chronik von Akakor (The Truth about the Chronicle of Akakor).*[6] This was done with my consent.

I'm just quoting the most important passages here. They are evidence for Tatunca Nara's change of mind:

FS (Ferdinand Schmid): *Tatunca, would you be so good and now explain to Mr. von Däniken why we cannot carry out the expedition by helicopter?*

TN (Tatunca Nara): *Well, you can fly to Kashmera (a waterfall). Look, my brother-in-law's people are about 5000 people scattered in the mountains. Now, if you come by helicopter, this would not only cause a great stir, it would create bad blood in the priesthood. The people would go crazy if a helicopter were to land in the middle of the mountains. It is just not possible. You have to travel from Kashmera by boat and then walk. You can do that in six days. . . . you take your camera equipment and whatever you need with you. And please take your time. Do not mark down certain days or weeks that you feel obligated to.*

EvD (Erich von Däniken): *Then we can forget about the expedition. We had planned to start now with* helicopters. *The new plan creates a completely new situation. I estimate that in this case, I would have to calculate an additional two to three months for it. Which I don't have because we have wasted time now. We have a variety of types of equipment with us, not just cameras. All this has to be transported . . .*

FS: *. . . Tatunca says it should be easy . . .*

TN: *Just come with me. Take your cameras and tape recorders with you. Drive up with me, cross the mountain, talk to my brother-in-law and the priest. You will see the devices and have your proof . . .*

EvD: *. . . No no! I have a commitment with German television on August 18.*

TN: *You have 130 days to appear in Akahim . . .*

EvD: *Just a moment! The original plan was to go by helicopter. We sent you to your people a few months ago and equipped you. It was agreed that you should bring us pictures and an item. You did not do that, Tatunca. We also organized everything for the helicopter expedition. That was not easy. And now you come here and say I have to go up there by boat and on foot. That's something else . . .*

TN: *Do you want to be shot down there by the gods?*

EvD: *. . . which gods should shoot me down and how?*

TN: *You will see. But now you are backing down.*

EvD: *If anyone is backing down here, it is you. Our expedition is fully planned and ready to take off. With helicopters.*

TN: *Your helicopter will crash. I can guarantee it, with my seal affixed.*

EvD: *... Three days ago, I spoke to researchers from the Max Planck Institute in Manaus. They told me they did not walk 50 meters into the jungle without marking their return path.*

TN: *Everything there is under water, there are constantly swamps and ants that fall from the trees. That's not the case in our mountains.*

EvD: *Why, Tatunca, did you say I have 130 days to go up there? Why exactly 130 days?*

TN: *130 days! No more compromises ...*

EvD: *... This creates a completely new situation, and I have to think carefully before I plunge into this adventure. This is not just about following you into the jungle.*

It is also about my international obligations. I also have a book project that I promised my publisher. And this manuscript must be ready before I disappear into the jungle. Also, I haven't got the slightest desire to just go up there without any plan, totally unorganized. I still insist that the expedition is being carried out with helicopters ... I do not see why a helicopter should make your people crazy like that. God knows, it's easy to land in a village square. An adventure and an experience for your tribesmen ...

TN: *As you wish. But you will have to come on foot.*

EvD: *I cannot see what confuses you about the helicopter. After all, there are also army helicopters flying*

around up there today. There are also airliners flying
over it.

TN: *But very high. In the helicopter, I cannot guaran-*
tee your life.

EvD: *But you already knew that. Mr. Schmid has*
explained to you that we are planning a helicopter
expedition.

TN: *But I did not know what kind of events have*
occurred in Akahim. These are the events of the gods.
Therefore, I can no longer give any guarantees.

EvD: *Events of the gods? What events?*

TN: *Let's just stay with what I've said so far.*

The next day Tatunca appeared and made a statement. Together with his brother-in-law he had encountered a stranger in the underground rooms. This is also
the reason why he was late coming to Manaus. His
brother-in-law had called the stranger "the Blessed
One" and had great respect for him. The Blessed One
wanted to know a great deal about the present state of
civilization, but also about Erich von Däniken. It had
been the Blessed One who had set the deadline of 130
days and banned a helicopter landing.

He, Tatunca, would now travel to Akahim and
bring back a piece of evidence for Erich von Däniken.
So that he would no longer have any doubts.

By that time, the whole Tatunca affair had cost me
around 80,000 Swiss Francs. This expense came from
the various flights between Switzerland and Brazil, for

technical equipment for Tatunca's boat (new engine) for an advance payment to the helicopter company, and for the fuel transport. After the conversation with Tatunca, I flew home and fulfilled my obligations. Ferdinand Schmid, however, traveled with Tatunca in his boat to the Kashmera de Alianza. This is a waterfall, where a house is located that Tatunca said he built with some helpers. On July 23, 1979, a telegram reached me:

AKAHIM EXISTS. CAPSIZED AT THE WATER-FALL. SAVED MY LIFE, EVERYTHING ELSE LOST. ALSO, PHOTOS, FILM DOCUMENTARY AND RELAXATION URGENTLY NEEDED. STORY WILL FOLLOW. GREETINGS FERDI.

Two weeks later, Ferdinand Schmid was in Switzerland and told me he had driven with Tatunca to the waterfall. Although this Tatunca is white-skinned, he moves like an indigenous person. He caught fish with his hands, strangled smaller crocodiles, and chopped off their tail with a machete. He knows every plant and every little vermin. Also, Tatunca knew exactly what was edible and what was inedible or poisonous. From the waterfall, Tatunca refused to continue with Ferdinand Schmid. One must know that Tatunca had kept a small boat ready on the Rio Padauari. Then, an incredibly strong rain storm set in. He, Ferdinand, capsized and fell into the water, fought for his life and lost all his equipment.

"But Ferdi, you telegraphed me that Akahim existed. How do you come to that conclusion?"

"Before the floods started, I saw a pyramid in the distance, about where Akahim was supposed to be. Not made of stone, but a pyramid overgrown with bushes. Definitely isosceles and no natural elevation. I've photographed them several times and I'm absolutely sure it's an artificial pyramid."

I let Ferdinand know that I didn't trust Tatunca. Something about his aura bothered me.

MURDER CHURNING

I would have to thoroughly think through any future endeavor. Tatunca had promised to bring me an item of that alien intelligence, straight from Akahim. The years passed, the object never came. I was asked to appear at the office of the Criminal Police in Aarau, Switzerland, and was questioned about Tatunca. Later, the Federal Criminal Police Department in Wiesbaden, Germany, asked me for information about him. I realized that he was probably a serial killer. Here are the cases that he might be responsible for:

=

In November 1980, 20-year-old John Reed from California met Tatunca Nara. Reed was a reckless adventurer. He trusted the "white Indian" who wanted to lead him to the legacies of aliens. Two weeks later, Tatunca returned alone. Asked about the whereabouts of Reed, he replied that Reed had molested Indian women while they were bathing and had therefore been shot dead with an arrow.

—

On November 13, 1983, 22-year-old forest ranger Herbert Wanner left his parents' home in Zofingen, Switzerland. In his baggage was a hunting rifle and a few hundred rounds of Brennecke ammunition. Wanner told his parents that he would be staying with his friend Tatunca Nara. Tatunca knew the young Wanner from an earlier trip. On December 10, 1983, Wanner's parents received a letter from their son. He confirmed his arrival at Tatunca's place. This was the last sign of life. On June 6, 1984, Wanner's worried parents received a letter written in German. Sender: Tatunca Nara. He told the parents that their son left in February. He wanted to cross the Amazon toward Venezuela, he said. The Wanners did not believe that. Their son would never undertake such an endeavor all by himself. And he had written to them before this.

But while man proposes, God disposes. Tatunca's lies were eventually revealed:

On July 7, 1984, a Swiss travel group flew to Brazil for an adventure trip (trekking) on the upper Amazon. Among the travelers were Swiss dentist Hans Kunz and his young wife. From Barcelos, the small group went on a river cruise on the Rio Araçá. At one point when the ship stopped for repairs, they were told by Indians working on the ship that only 800 meters further up the river was a human skeleton. Dr. Kunz had them show him the spot and found the bones. In the back of skull was a bullet hole. Dr. Kunz put the fully preserved lower jaw and fragments of the upper jaw in his travel bag. Another trekking participant found a projectile at the site, later identified as a Brennecke bullet. And just a few feet from the skeleton, Dr. Kunz found a cap. Inside was the inscription *S.A. Fabrica di Capelli Bellinzona* (in German, *Hutfabrik Bellinzona AG*, a hat factory in Bellinzona, Switzerland).

Back in Switzerland, Dr. Kunz forwarded his macabre find to the city police in Zurich, together with the projectile and the cap. After all, Bellinzona was a town in the Swiss canton of Ticino, and therefore the dead man could be Swiss. After several months of forensic research, the answers were available: The skeleton clearly belonged to Herbert Wanner. His killer had shot him with his own ammunition from behind.

=

The third murder case concerns a personal acquaintance of mine: Mrs. Christine Heuser, a woman with German-Swedish dual citizenship. She had been a participant in a group trip to Egypt that I had led. During group tours, people often chat at the bar in the evening, and Christine heard about Tatunca Nara for the first time in our company. Back home, she bought *Die Chronik von Akakor* (*The Chronicle of Akakor*) by Karl Brugger. The book fascinated her.

Mrs. Heuser was a lovable and humorous lady. Professionally, she ran a yoga school, and she firmly believed that she had lived during a former life on the Amazon River. She got the idea to fly to Manaus and, if possible, visit Tatunca Nara. We urged her to forget this absurd idea, with no success. Christine kept reiterating that she was independent and an adult. In addition, she was a yoga teacher and used to do Japanese jiu-jitsu, a type of martial art. Christine flew to Manaus in the summer of 1987—and never came back. Subsequent inquiries revealed that Christine Heuser had indeed met Tatunca. Tatunca had told Ferdinand Schmid that he had gone with her to Kashmera, but that she wanted to have sex with him. He was not interested and insisted that she return to Manaus. But she never arrived there.

═

The fourth, and most mysterious, case concerns Brazilian Felicitas Barreto. I had corresponded with her since 1970, but in the fall of 1971, we met personally in Teresina, Brazil. Felicitas Barreto was an ethnologist without an academic title. Her research included several tribes, such as the Kuna, Chocó, Guaymies, and the Tiryó Indians. Her fate was sealed by a coincidence. As a young nurse, Felicitas had been a passenger in a small plane that had to make an emergency landing where the Taulipang Indians live. When she jumped out of the plane, she broke her ankle. The tribe's medicine man healed the injury, and Felicitas lived with the Taulipang for seven full years. After returning to Rio de Janeiro, she sent FUNAI to *Ilha do Bananal*

(Bananal Island) to provide medical assistance to the local Indians.

When we met in Teresina on October 12, 1971, her luggage was full of notes, bones, and skulls she found in a cave in the Tumucumaque Mountains. The walls of the cave, according to Felicitas, are filled with inexplicable signs. Through her research she wrote a manuscript called *Requiem für die Indianer* (*Requiem for the Indians*).[7] It is still in my archive today. We could not find a publisher.

My correspondence with Felicitas was quite extensive. I also briefed her on my connections with Tatunca Nara and about the planned expedition to Akahim. She let me know that she also wanted to pursue this matter seriously. Felicitas Barreto spoke several Indian dialects. The jungle was her second home. I was not worried about her getting along with the Indians or the

FIGURE 4.3: *Felicitas Barreto and Erich von Däniken*

environment there. Her last letter reached me on September 29, 1985. Of several letters that I subsequently sent her, one came back with the note: unknown. Had she also found out about Tatunca's secret?

—

And finally, there is the murder of Karl Brugger. Killed with several shots. Murders happen in Rio every day, but they are usually robberies. Brugger's killer did not care about his victim's cash. He did not reach into a pocket.

TATUNCA'S EXPOSURE

Who is this Tatunca Nara? The Federal Criminal Police Department in Wiesbaden explained it to me.

—

Günther Hauck, aka Tatunca Nara, was born on October 5, 1941, in Grub am Forst in Bavaria, the son of a porcelain painter. A few months after his birth, his father died in the war in Stalingrad, and his mother died of cancer in 1955. Hauck, together with his two older sisters, came to an orphanage. After completing elementary school, Hauck began an apprenticeship as a bricklayer, but he didn't stick with it. On January 10, 1966, Hauck disappeared from Germany. It turned out that he had signed on to work on a ship that was heading for South America.

On June 4, 1966, Hauck was taken into custody by order of the captain of the *Dorthe Oldendorff* by the police in La Guaira, Venezuela. Because of mental abnormalities, he ended up in a psychiatric hospital. Dr. Nikolai Jerums in Caracas, Venezuela, who examined him, diagnosed him with a schizoid psychopathy—a split personality. At that time, Hauck was already claiming that he was an Indian whose tribe lived in the upper Amazon. Hauck soon fled the psychiatric hospital but was picked up again by the authorities in Venezuela in mid-1967. On November 27, 1967, he was handed over to the German Embassy, accompanied by a medical officer, and was transferred back to (West) Germany.

Then on February 15, 1968, he got a job at a Hamburg shipping company and sailed with the *Luise Bornhofen* to Rio de Janeiro. On December 12, 1968, he left the ship without permission and without checking out. He soon emerged in Brazil and acted as a guide for tour groups and researchers. After he freed some Brazilian air force officers from the hands of Indians, he received a Brazilian passport in the name of Tatunca Nara, and that document also identified him as an Indian. Since 1972, Tatunca Nara, aka Günther Hauck, has been living with Mrs. Anita Katz. Mrs. Katz is Brazilian, but descends from German-born Jews. She studied medicine and law, and from time to time, she worked as a physician in Barcelos. She has also worked as a public prosecutor.

——

As of April 2015 (when I typed these lines) Tatunca Nara should be 74 years old. In Barcelos, a small town on the Rio Negro, lives a son of his. His name is Seder Helio. He does not speak German anymore. He told the German news magazine *Der Spiegel*: "My father may have said a lot of nonsense. But he is my father. None of the allegations of murder have ever been proven."[8] Why has Tatunca never been arrested? The Federal Criminal Police Department in Wiesbaden planned to, but they had to stop the proceedings, because one cannot prosecute a genuine or false Indian living somewhere high up in the mountains at the end of the world. Tatunca is also the legitimate owner of a Brazilian passport. And his wife also worked as a state attorney. She is probably very familiar with the tedious paperwork of the authorities on the upper Amazon.

And Ferdinand Schmid? He returned to Switzerland to live in an apartment in Gossau. The older he got, the more he believed he would receive "psychotelepathic messages from the heavenly spheres." Copies of such communications landed regularly on my desk. Until his death, Ferdinand Schmid was convinced of the existence of Akahim. "Tatunca might have told the most outrageous lies," he said, "but I saw and photographed the pyramid at the height of Akahim. Nobody can take that away from me."

CONNECTION TO ECUADOR?

A mysterious city with underground spaces, with treasures and writings of a foreign culture, also exists in Ecuador. Who knows, maybe Tatunca Nara's Akahim is identical to the location of the so-called Metal Library of Ecuador. This underground system is also associated with (at least) one murder. That of Señor Petronio Jaramillo Abarca who was gunned down (a detailed report about this crime is in *Falsch Informiert (Misinformed!)*).[9] Prior to his murder, Abarca was the only surviving eyewitness who personally visited these underground facilities. We knew each other. He reported that to gain access, he and two colleagues had to dive through a river and that they came out in a cave. Down there, in different rooms, he saw "thousands of animal figures, of chimeras, of crystal-like pillars in different colors, and finally a metal library with thousands upon thousands of pages."[10] Every metal folio is about 40×20 inches in size. And the space is lit by a hazy, artificial light whose source he could not determine. Abarca, who had said he wanted to visit me in Switzerland, was shot dead on May 18, 1998, outside his home in Esmeraldas, Ecuador. Just like that. As with Karl Brugger, it was not a robbery.

And where should this treasure of an unknown, possibly even alien culture lie? Exactly at 77° 47' 34" west and 1° 56' 00" south. Several teams have tried to reach this geographic point to finally film the unique treasures. Scotsman Stanley Hall failed due to the weather and the wrong equipment, Ecuadorian journalist Alex Chiontti failed because of the Shuar, a local Indian tribe that tolerates no strangers in holy places.[11] Are these Shuar possibly identical to Tatunca's Mongulalas?

What needs to be noted is that previous efforts to gain the technological legacy of extraterrestrial intelligence have been unsuccessful. No alien technology is in my vault. Now the idea of finding a piece of technology from a strange solar system on our good old Earth is not as absurd as it originally seemed. The ark of the Bible could be alien technology, for instance. This is at least stated in the Bible and in the Ethiopian *Buch der Könige* (*Book of Kings*).[12] And at the interfaith meeting on June 19, 2009, the head of the Ethiopian Orthodox Church, Patriarch Abune Paulos, confirmed the following in Rome, "Yes. The Ark of the Covenant is in Aksum. I have seen it. It wasn't made by humans."[13]

PADRE LE PAIGE AND THE TOMBS OF ALIENS

Another eyewitness to the impossible was Belgian Padre Gustavo Le Paige. He lived in Chile for decades. The padre was active not only as a clergyman, but also as an archaeologist. In mid-April 1975, the journalist Juan Abarzua reported the following:

> The Belgian clergyman Gustavo Le Paige is convinced that human-like creatures from other planets have been buried on our Earth. Padre Le Paige has been carrying out archeological research for 20 years. The 72-year-old missionary priest has uncovered 5,424

gravesites... "Some of the mummies had facial shapes that one doesn't find on Earth."

The padre also said that people would not believe him if he told them what else he found in the graves.[14]

The Swiss Embassy in Santiago, Chile, had arranged a meeting between me and the padre. Padre Le Paige knew of some of my books. We were to meet in Santiago on May 28, 1980. Only days before the very important conversation with me, however, the clergyman died.

The situation is sometimes really like a curse. On May 28, 1978, a Reverend C. Scarborough, from Cape Town, South Africa, wrote to me and said that he had lived for many years on Kiribati, a group of islands in

FIGURE 4.4: Padre Le Paige

the Pacific, and that he also spoke the native language there:

> *The first thing that bothered me was the fact that the islanders use two words for human. They call themselves* Aomata, *which means "man of this earth." But they call people of skin color other than their own* Te I-Matang, *which literally translates as "Man from the land of the Gods."*

Through further correspondence with Reverend Scarborough, I learned that on one of the islands of Kiribati there were graves of giants. Aliens? I wondered. I asked Reverend Scarborough. He strongly recommended that I visit Kiribati. He said his successor there was Father Kamoriki, and that he would be very happy to help me.

Father Kamoriki died two days before I landed on Kiribati. Jinxed?[15]

THE DISCOVERY OF THE BAND OF HOLES

It does not have to be murder or natural death to get sensitive information in South America. Often the paths are crooked. Thus, in the fall of 1978, an elderly gentleman showed me two aerial photographs. This took place in the foyer of a hotel in Chicago, where the Fifth World Conference of the AAS was taking place. The stranger asked if I knew what the aerial photographs showed. He had cut them out of an old *National Geographic*. I looked at the black-and-white pictures taken with a wide-angle lens. They showed a panorama of a hilly, furrowed landscape. Presumably this was taken somewhere in the foothills, because the ground bore scars of gravelly mountain streams. There was no vegetation in the picture. Not a tree, not a shrub. But there was a strange, black trail that went down a hill.

"Do you know this place? Do you know where that is?" The stranger asked.

"Never seen it!" I responded.

The man slid a second photo into my hands—an enlargement of the dark track. I saw the same curious line over the hills, only this time I recognized holes punched into the terrain, as if they had been left here by an overpowering roller. I used the usual width of mountain streams as a reference point and estimated the width of this strange track to be about 15 meters. It was about then that the old black and white pictures began to excite me.

"Do you have any idea where these pictures were taken?" I asked the well-groomed gentleman.

He did not know anything specific, but he did know that National Geographic had shown these pictures in connection to a story about Peru but the magazine had not provided a name for the place.

At home, I rummaged through some books on Peru, hoping to find the pictures. But they did not show up anywhere. An inquiry to *National Geographic* in Washington, DC, did not help. They told me the photos were decades old and the photographer had died long ago. So I kept looking and found books about

Peru with pictures of the great Inca wall. It winds from the coastal land near Paramonga up into the Peruvian mountains. It is 60 kilometers long. But I quickly figured out that what I was looking for was not this Inca wall. Finally, I sent letters to my Peruvian acquaintances, always with photocopies of the two black and white pictures from the old *National Geographic*. I was about to give up when I received an answer from Air Force Colonel Omar Chioino Carranza. I knew him pretty well. He had been the driving force behind the construction of an aeronautical museum in Lima. The colonel wrote that he had circulated my pictures among his fellow airmen, and the holey track was located in the Andes foothills northeast of the city of Trujillo.

—

On August 15, 1980, Colonel Carranza and I met in the lobby of the Sheraton in Lima. We sat down at a marble table and ordered the customary Pisco Sour (a mixed drink of pisco, lemon, sugar, egg whites, and a dash of Angostura bitters).

"I've prepared everything," the colonel said after exchanging private information. "Tomorrow morning at 6:00 the Land Rover will be ready. If all goes well, you can be back in four days. My friend Frederico Falconi, an archaeologist, will accompany you. He knows *la Murella* very well . . ."

"*La Murella* means wall, doesn't it?" The error dawned on me, and I sensed the small, big difference.

"Of course!" said Colonel Carranza. "You want to see it?"

Used to grief, the misunderstanding hit me hard, but it did not discourage me. For the umpteenth time I pulled from my shoulder bag the old *National Geographic* images.

"Amigo, I want to see that! The wall is unimportant."

For a second the colonel twirled his mustache, begged forgiveness, got up, and went to the telephone booth beside the reception desk. Shortly thereafter, he returned and said that he had cancelled the Land Rover and the archaeologists but that he had reached architect Carlos Milla. He said Carlos knew every archaeological curiosity in the country, including the unofficial ones. He was a grave robber and a trader of stolen goods. May God protect him.

—

A week later I met Carlos Milla. Again at the Sheraton in Lima. Milla was a polite man, he only spoke when spoken to. His rough hands signaled that he was used to physical work.

"You know what I'm looking for," I said without any small talk. "Please show me on the map where to find this curious band of holes in the field."

"Si, yes, Señor. I know exactly where it is, down to the meter. I can draw it on the map."

"Please do!" I encouraged him.

The grave robber closed his eyes, opened them, and sent a help-seeking look to Colonel Carranza, who was also there, tapping his fingers nervously on the tabletop. Turning to me, he said quietly in English, "I believe he wants money!"

I have long been accustomed to having to fork out cash in all developing countries. Cash is king. I shoved a $100 bill along with his Pisco Sour glass across the table. "Please, where is it?"

Carlos Milla examined the bill. He wanted more. In order to get to the information, he himself had expenses, he said. He would also accompany me. I explained to him that accompaniment was unnecessary, that I had friends in the country. For $600, we were trading.

Milla finally gave me the information I was looking for: "Your band of holes reaches much further over mountains and valleys than the old *National Geographic* pictures show. The most convenient spot for you to access it is 2 kilometers beyond the village of Humay in the Pisco Valley. Drive to Hacienda Montesierpe. In the sloping terrain behind the hacienda is a 300-meter-wide strip of cultivated land. Just above it, you'll find your strange holey band."

The information was correct. Dr. Janvier Cabrera accompanied me on the first trip. He lived in the Peruvian city of Ica, not far from the Pisco Valley. At close range, the holes turned out to be small, round walls, and there were always eight in a row. Their original meaning is still unknown, but you can read more about this in one of my other books entitled *Grüße aus der Steinzeit (Evidence of the Gods)*.[16] Thanks to my books, many tourist groups now visit this Band of Holes. From Dr. Cabrera,

I also learned how, for centuries, the locals have called these strange holes *La Avenida misteriosa de las picaduras de viruelas*—the enigmatic street of pockmarks.

BRIBED WITH A TOBACCO PIPE AND A HELI-FLIGHT INTO THE UNKNOWN

Once I even managed to bribe a real general of the Colombian Air Force—not with money, but with a special gift. This is what happened:

On February 1, 1981, the German news magazine Der Spiegel printed the following article: "Indio-Kultur im Dschungel" ("Indian Culture in the Jungle").[17] From it, I learned that in the Colombian jungle, mysterious cities of a lost culture had been discovered whose builders had a special relationship to the universe. This is the opinion of the chief excavator of these cities, a professor of archeology at Universidad de los Andes in Bogotá named Dr. Alvaro Soto Holguín. I found that the excavation area was sealed off by the military, so I wrote to this professor and asked for more information. All my letters went unanswered. I began to think that maybe the man had something against me. Finally, I wrote to attorney Dr. Miguel Forerro for help—I had been using Forerro's help with correspondence for some time.

Forerro responded promptly. I should come to Bogotá, he wrote. Apparently, in Colombia, only personal encounters are acceptable. In fact, Forerro managed to bring Dr. Holguín and me together. We met several times at his university. Dr. Holguín is a gracious scholar who answered my questions in detail and even confessed to having read three of my books. "The city in the jungle is called Buritaca 200. We also call it *La cuidad perdida*, The Lost City. It is located in the Sierra Nevada range of Santa Marta and stretches between 32° 50' and 74° 15' to the west of Greenwich."

I learned that the area was huge. The Lost City alone is ten times larger than the well-known Inca fortress of Machu Picchu in Peru. "How do you get there?" I asked.

"By donkey or horse the trip takes five days or you can get there by helicopter, but you cannot rent a helicopter anywhere. The mountains around the Caribbean city of Santa Marta are dominated by drug lords. It produces Santa Marta Gold, the best quality marijuana in South America. That's why the military is present, but the military also works together with the drug bosses."

Nice prospects, I thought, but all of this made me feel even stronger about going there. Thanks to Dr. Forerro's connections, I made contact with some helicopter pilots at a lecture in the officers' club of the FAC (*Fuerza Aerea Columbiano*). The pilots listened to me attentively and asked many interesting questions. During the ensuing dinner, I asked around the room, "Gentlemen, how do I get to Buritaca 200, the Lost City?"

The officers gave me a rather blank look. "Where are you going?" a young captain said. I clearly felt that Buritaca 200 didn't mean much more to the pilots than any tiny village. Although they had heard of the Lost City, no one knew where it was located. Because of the information I gained from Dr. Holguín, I was able to tell the astonished Colombians the exact geographical position of the destination.

Over the obligatory black coffee after dinner, Five-Star Air Force General Paredes Diago asked me what type of strange tobacco pipe I was always sucking on. He noted that he was a passionate pipe collector but he had never come across my type of pipe. The pipe I used to smoke did not have the bent, classic pipe bowl. The tobacco was kept in a small, lattice-sealed container that was a direct extension of the mouth piece. The annoying, constant refilling during smoking was eliminated because I could easily press the glowing tobacco back into the container by applying gentle pressure.

FIGURE 4.7: *The pipe with which I bribed the air force general*

General Diago held my pipe in his hand, examining it from all sides.

"What does it cost?" he asked.

"Not for sale!" I replied. "But I'll get you a new one for a helicopter ride to Buritaca 200."

For a moment, the general looked at me thoughtfully. Then he asked his adjutant which unit was in Santa Marta and whether the battalion had helicopters. An hour later I held a written general order in my hands:

FUERZA AEREA COLUMBIANA. Señor Teniente Coronel. Hector Lopez Ramirez Commandante Batallon de Infantria No 5 Cordova Santa Marta.

El Señor Erich von Däniken esats autorizado por este Commando para efectuar un vuelo en Helicotero Hughes que se encuentra en esa Unidad, de la cuidad Santa Marta a la cuidan perdida.

Cordial saluto, General Raul Alberto Paredes Diago, Commandante Fuerza Aerea.

(The translation goes something like this: To Colonel Hector Lopez Ramirez, Commander of the Fifth Infantry Battalion in Cordova Santa Marta. Mr. Erich von Däniken is authorized by this order to carry out a flight with helicopter *Hughes*, which is in your unit, from Santa Marta to the Lost City.)

This is how I reached the Lost City in the jungle and was the first reporter to publish a detailed picture report. Read about it in *Unmögliche Wahrheiten (Impossible Truths)*.[18]

THE TREASURES OF CARLOS CRESPI

Without the support of wonderful and generous people, I would never have achieved many of my goals, and I would never have been able to write/report about the Lost City in Colombia, the Band of Holes in Peru, or the treasures of Father Carlos Crespi in Ecuador.

Who is Father Crespi and what role did he play in relation to the early history of man?

I have to thank speleologist and prospector Juan Moricz for enabling my first visit with Father Crespi. The same Juan Moricz was the one who told the world about the underground metal library. In late March 1972, Juan took me to the Ecuadorian city of Cuenca and headed straight for the Catholic Church of *Maria Auxiliadore* (the Church of the Helpful Mother of God). Father Crespi and Moricz hugged each other like old friends, then the priest hugged me as well. Father Crespi, I was told, was originally a Salesian priest before his order called him to Cuenca. The elevation of the place is about 2500 meters up in the Ecuadorian Andes. When I met him, Father Crespi was in charge of the Cuenca Catholic community. This was his charge for over 60 years, and he enjoyed a reputation of being a trusted friend of the Indians. Even during his lifetime, the natives already regarded him as a saint. He has since died, but a monument has been erected in his honor, which is decorated with fresh flowers every day. What was so special about this priest? He listened to the Indians for hours, even days. He gained their trust and helped them in every conceivable life situation, often going against the Ecuadorian state power.

The Indians returned the favor and gave the good-natured, not exactly well-groomed priest works of art that their families had hidden from the whites for centuries. Father Crespi first placed these on the walls of his inner courtyard, and when he received more, he piled them up in a shed behind the church. But the gifts continued to arrive, so Father Crespi opened two more rooms, which contained some of the most amazing things I have ever seen.

On my first visit in March 1972—I met him two more times later on—he wanted to hold the objects in his own hands, but I was allowed to photograph them. Anything that shone in golden colors was pure gold to the clergyman. "Come, Erich, come!" He shouted, pulling me to the next surprise. "Es oro! Oro puro!" ("It's gold, pure gold!"), he said again and again, holding the next treasure under my nose. Since the priest did not want to give up the objects, I could never estimate their weight. So later I wrote about "brass, copper, zinc, tin, stone and woodwork, and among all this clutter real gold, gold foil, silver and sheet silver."[19]

Today, having had time to gain knowledge about such things, I know that weight and color have nothing to do with the gold content of an object. How can this be true? Dr. Heather Lechtman, director of the Center for Materials Research in Archeology and Ethnology

at the Massachusetts Institute of Technology sent me
her research report, which states:

> *In our laboratory, we analyzed small samples of dis-*
> *covered pieces. It turned out that the coating was often*
> *only about 0.5 to two microns thin and was, even in*
> *microscopic images with up to 500-fold magnification,*
> *barely noticeable ... The rulers of the Inca empire used*
> *objects that look like pure gold or silver. Their methods*
> *of surface refinement, with which the inhabitants of*
> *America in pre-Columbian times give non-precious*
> *metal pieces the appearance of precious metal, are*
> *unequaled."*[20]

Dr. Gebhardt, 1972 director of the Max Planck
Institute for Metals Research in Stuttgart, who for
decades dealt with the metallurgical knowledge of
the Inca and pre-Inca and is regarded as a first-class
expert, also confirmed to me that the "weight and color
of an object does not tell anything about its actual gold
content."[21]

Because of my reporting on Father Crespi's treasures, I was later attacked countless times. In Germany, an entire book was published against me, in
which, of course, I was once more "unmasked, refuted,
convicted."[22] Critics overlooked the fact that American
archaeologist Dr. J. Mason Valentine, honorary cura-
tor of the Miami Museum of Science and a research
member of the Honolulu Bishop Museum, considered
the same Crespi artifacts that I had published about
to be genuine. Archeology writer Charles Berlitz also
published pictures from the Crespi collection.[23] But

the rest of the science community was silent. Well, I understand that archaeologists are also only human beings, and I understand that people like to look away or judge very rashly when archaeological treasures do not fit into their scheme. The Crespi collection does not fit in anywhere. It contains metal plates with pyramids, and at the pyramids' bases is clearly visible writing, signs that no human ever deciphered. Both stone and metal plates repeatedly show different writings and elephants. But there were never any elephants in South America.

I photographed a bewildering array of images of giraffe-like creatures, with heads from which rays emanate, with monkey-like scared faces from which snakes grow, as well as gilded panels divided into 56 blocks with a character in each block.[24]

But all of these artifacts are dismissed as modern counterfeits. As if simple, poor Indians who live in small village communities in the highlands of Ecuador and do not even know the alphabet would invent strange characters and then stamp them on expensive metal, coated with gold and silver, during their poverty-ridden lives. In addition, the art direction that presented itself to me in the Crespi collection must be from a pre-Christian period. Why? Nowhere did the alleged Indian counterfeiters affix a cross, a Madonna, a baby Jesus, a manger, an ascension, or any Christian motif. The faces and grimaces on the metal plates are strange, the whole style doesn't fit any existing art history, and it doesn't stem from an illustrated magazine.

The alleged counterfeits have also been stamped into metal plates coated with the same perfect coating method used in pre-Inca times. These methods involved incredible melting and alloying processes in which 50 percent copper, 25 percent silver, and 25 percent gold were mixed to form micro-thin alloys—a process that today's Indians are not aware of. In their material poverty, they could have neither afforded the smelting furnaces nor the casting technology, let alone the expensive raw material.

The experts who should actually deal with this collection are looking away. They label the artifacts as forgeries rather than dealing with the Crespi collection scientifically. They also overlook the fact that Father Crespi served as chairman of the Cuenca Gold Museum until July 20, 1962. It was then that the museum burnt down and many artifacts landed back at the church of *Maria Auxiliadore*. So it is only when the objects were displayed behind bulletproof glass in the gold museum that they were considered genuine?! After Crespi died, the state collected most of the artifacts from the his collection. Allegedly, a new gold museum is to be built.

I think the neglect of the Crespi collection is an archeological disgrace. Scholars do not want to acknowledge that the history of the pre-Inca tribes was quite different than what they previously taught. The same statement applies as in regard to UFOs or the Jesus grave in Srinagar: the world does not give a damn. It is supposed to remain misinformed and ignorant.

CHAPTER 5

Hidden Connections

In which you will learn about the following:

Over There They Think Differently • In Which Universities? • How AAS Was Founded • Praise and Scathing Review • Crash Go the Chariots • Hypocritical Critics • Clifford Wilson and His Background • Reconciliation with G. G. • Inside Space Command • Secret Lecture at NASA • International Relations Networks

On September 14, 1973, the American lawyer Gene Phillips founded The Ancient Astronaut Society (AAS) in Chicago as a nonprofit, international society that engages with my topics. How did this come about? And who is Dr. Gene Phillips? Was he allowed to found this company, and what is his relationship with me?

The question, "Did Earth receive visits from outer space thousands of years ago?" is an interesting one for every thinking human being. After all, it's about studying crucial knowledge with regard to the following points:

- Emergence of life in the universe
- Emergence of life and intelligence on Earth
- Reasons for the origin of religion
- Origins of global traditions
- Descriptions of gods in old sacred and unholy texts
- Descriptions of technical equipment and technical operations in ancient texts
- Imitation cults, known as cargo cults, of prehistoric peoples
- Astronomical findings of simple tribal societies
- Legendary prehistoric gods, primal emperors, and forefathers of the ancient peoples
- Disappearance of many religious and mythological figures into "heaven"
- The promise of the return in many religions and cultures
- Time-shifting effects mentioned in various ancient texts
- Motivation for many inexplicable buildings of antiquity
- Astonishing similarities of many world-wide formations and drawings
- Symbolism of godly figures and representations

- The worldwide phenomenon of huge images that are visible only from the sky

All these topics are dealt with by the Ancient Astronaut Society—and by me. It only makes sense that I, as the most exposed figure of this organization, am internationally attacked and laughed at, but also admired. It's like in politics. Some love you; others want you to go to hell.

OVER THERE THEY THINK DIFFERENTLY

This is why I have been holding lectures internationally for decades—in public, in secret societies, and at universities. In the US, the scientific climate is different than it is in good old Europe. US society is fundamentally more open, more curious, more spontaneous than the European one. It is also less obedient—at least in the scientific field. The fact that the NSA (National Security Agency) can spy on anyone lately has not changed this basic statement. In the US, anyone can choose the answer that makes sense to them; in Europe, on the other hand, we find a kind of scientific dictatorship.

IN WHICH UNIVERSITIES?

Below is an abbreviated list of the universities where I have held lectures and discussions in the United States:

- University of California, San Francisco, California

- North Adams State College (now the Massachusetts College of Liberal Arts), North Adams, Massachusetts
- University of Pittsburgh, Pittsburgh, Pennsylvania
- Eastern Illinois University, Charleston, Illinois
- Illinois Institute of Technology, Chicago, Illinois
- University of Missouri, Columbia, Missouri
- Middle Tennessee State University, Murfreesboro, Tennessee
- University of Georgia, Athens, Georgia
- University of West Florida, Pensacola, Florida
- University of Texas at El Paso, El Paso, Texas
- New Mexico State University, Las Cruces, New Mexico
- Texas Christian University, Fort Worth, Texas
- University of New Mexico, Albuquerque, New Mexico
- University of Tennessee, Knoxville, Tennessee
- University of Nebraska Omaha, Omaha, Nebraska
- Minnesota State University, Mankato, Minnesota
- Georgia State University, Atlanta, Georgia

- Tennessee Tech University, Cookeville, Tennessee
- Eastern Kentucky University, Richmond, Kentucky
- University of West Virginia, Morgantown, West Virginia
- The University of Utah, Salt Lake City, Utah
- University of New Hampshire, Durham, New Hampshire
- University at Buffalo, Buffalo, New York
- University of Nevada, Las Vegas, Nevada
- Georgia Institute of Technology, Atlanta, Georgia
- Illinois State University, Normal, Illinois
- University of North Carolina at Chapel Hill, Chapel Hill, North Carolina
- New York Institute of Technology, New York, New York
- City University of New York, New York, New York
- Harvard University, Cambridge, Massachusetts

In contrast, invitations to speak at European universities are one-off occasions. (The last lecture I held at a university was on April 28, 2015, at the Faculty of Religious Studies at the University of Friborg, Switzerland.)

HOW AAS WAS FOUNDED

After I delivered a lecture at the University of Chicago, a friendly looking, short-statured gentleman spoke to me. He introduced himself as Gene Phillips, a lawyer. Could he invite me to have a glass of wine with him? I learned that his area of expertise was medical litigation. In the US, you call each other by first names rather quickly after you've introduced yourselves.

"Erich," he said, "your topic is so intriguing and encompassing that you'll never be able to do it alone. The whole thing is interdisciplinary; it reaches all across society and science."

He was right. Gene, as I called him from then on, suggested an Erich von Däniken Society. That's exactly what I did not want. A research society, yes, but it should not carry my name. Why not? In the 1970s, I was even more controversial than I am today, when the waves have calmed down to some extent. An Erich von Däniken Society would have been torn apart by the prevailing zeitgeist. It had to be another name. This is what I made clear to Dr. Gene Phillips.

We met several times. Gene proved to be a person of integrity. I met his family—his wife, sons, and daughters. He had his area of expertise, the law, well under control. On the evening of July 16, 1973, he said, "I have a suggestion. How about the Ancient Astronaut Society?" The term told me nothing, initially. *Ancient Astronauts*? Wouldn't that mean "old astronauts"? Gene clarified this for me. In this case *ancient* meant prehistoric astronauts. I was all in. That's how the Ancient Astronaut Society came about.

Gene Phillips and I became friends. Now retired, he lives with his wife Doris, a native of Peru, in Florida. The American Ancient Astronaut Society is now called AAS-RA (Ancient Astronaut Society Research Association), is managed by Giorgio Tsoukalos in California, and publishes the magazine *Legendary Times*. The parent company remained in my hands. We still call ourselves AAS, but now this refers to the Society for Archeology, Astronautics, and SETI (which stands for the search for extraterrestrial intelligence). Every two months, our trade magazine *Sagenhafte Zeiten* (*Legendary Times*) is published. This magazine has an open contribution policy; find out more at the end of this book.

PRAISE, SCATHING REVIEWS, AND THE *CRASH GO THE CHARIOTS*

After my movie, *Erinnerungen an die Zukunft* (which translates to *Memories of the Future* but which was released as *Chariots of the Gods* in the US), aired eight times on US television from coast to coast, and after my book, *Chariots of the Gods*, climbed to number one on all bestseller lists, a new virus, according to the *New York Times*, broke out: Dänikenitis. At the same time, an anti-Däniken book was published: *Crash Go the Chariots*.[1] It was a scathingly negative review. It basically said that everything I've written is inventions, lies, and misunderstandings. It claims that I do not understand anything about archeology and that I disregard the respected interpretations of leading scholars. It says the desert of Nazca in Peru has never been an airport, as I claim, and that the grave plate of Palenque in Mexico shows no aliens at all, simply a Mayan prince named Pacal. It goes on to say that the biblical prophet Ezekiel never described a spaceship, but was allowed to experience a divine vision, which has been clearly demonstrated by several influential theologians. In fact, it claims that my biblical digressions were like devil's work. In addition, supposedly I am a plagiarist because French authors Louis Pauwels and Jaques Bergier already dealt with these topics long before me, and it goes on and on. All in all, *Crash Go the Chariots* actually crashed a lot. Its publication left my credibility and reputation in tatters. In addition, many American newspapers highly praised anti-Däniken author Clifford Wilson. "Finally," they were cheering, "a professor of archeology unmasked this amateur Däniken." It was high time for a scientist to put Däniken's nonsense in perspective, they thought. And, of course, religious magazines labeled me as an atheist.

Suddenly, Erich von Däniken, admired for his courage, had been pushed off the pedestal overnight.

HYPOCRITICAL CRITICS, CLIFFORD WILSON AND HIS BACKGROUND, AND A RECONCILIATION WITH G. G.

Just who was this Däniken disprover? This Dr. Clifford Wilson, Professor of Archeology? At which university did he teach? I asked my publisher, Putnam Books in New York, but those in charge found no answers and said anti-books would help the discussion and not hurt the circulation. But they hurt my reputation. And so began a fight against distortions and misunderstandings, which I have been allowed to conduct in several languages since then. The bona fide layman does not suspect with which methods in books, on TV, and, of course, on the Internet things are falsified, how everything is completely turned around. I don't like to count the programs anymore, but as I am attacked the most, I am entitled to take a stand against the plot of stupidity.

None of my books say that Nazca was the "space airport of the gods." In addition, I covered all Nazca theories in detail.[2] Scratched drawings are constantly being presented to audiences in TV programs that are broadcast worldwide, and viewers are led to believe that these narrow lines, all part of figures, are the true mystery of Nazca. But remember, images are shamelessly manipulated. The real sensation you get at of Nazca are not those narrow lines, but the slope-like trapezes and artificially flattened mountains. I have documented this in my books with countless pictures. Pictures, by the way, that are not shown by any TV station.

Another point of disagreement surrounds the grave plate of Palenque, Mexico. The experts are right in their view that it does not show an alien, but rather Pacal, the second-to-last ruler of the Mayan city. But Pacal is shown driving toward outer space. Every little detail on the phenomenal plate has to do with the universe. This is also confirmed by the most recent research undertaken by Maya researchers.[3] But in the hypocritical anti-Däniken broadcasts, you don't hear anything about this. "Scientific enlightenment" is supposed to be carried out scientifically—instead, these concoctions are sloppy. Everyone who is familiar with the subject matter will instantly see through the nonsense, but the layman has no idea and must accept what is presented to him.

In the worst programs, it seems as if the person in charge of producing the TV program does not know which image belongs with which text. And the editorial producer is not the same person who interviewed me, so it should not be surprising if images and narrative don't match up. For example, in a broadcast, the narrator might talk in an objective voice—of course!—about an underground crypt in Dendera, Egypt. But while they're doing this, the camera shows a robot driving along the so-called "ascending corridor" of the Great Pyramid. One has as little to do with the other as the Yeti has to do with a Catholic high altar. Or the image on screen might show Mayan pyramids in Central America, but the speaker is talking about the Incas in South America.

Or some buffoon claims that I admitted in an interview that I had manipulated pictures and text in my books. Sorry! I don't stoop to such nonsense. Sentences I spoke at some time and some place are taken out of context, reassembled, and reinterpreted. It's like endless ping-pong—produced by and for the poor in spirit.

Dr. Clifford Wilson even blamed me for things that I didn't actually write. Oh yes, the prophet Ezekiel in the Bible did not experience a vision of the Lord, but an extraterrestrial shuttle. I still stand by it today and can also support it objectively.[4] And am I a plagiarist? Even years before my book *Chariots of the Gods,* I wrote in various newspapers about my later book topics. For example, in 1964, the Canadian newspaper *The Northwest* published a full-page article of mine titled "Did Our Ancestors Visit Space?"[5] It is no secret that other authors have tackled the same topic. I correctly listed all of my colleagues in the reference section of *Chariots of the Gods.* When fruits are ripe, they fall from the tree at the same time. This also applies to the respective zeitgeist.

Years passed after the publication of *Crash Go the Chariots.* I published new books and admitted to some mistakes that I never repeated. At some point in the 1980s, I was a guest on a TV discussion forum in Sidney, Australia. With me at the table was the long-sought anti-Däniken professor Dr. Clifford Wilson. Finally! He was a very friendly gentleman, who expressed himself affectionately and unctuously. We did not argue in front of the camera, but held an objective conversation. Afterward, over a drink, I inquired at which university he was teaching archeology. And what his special field was. Ancient Sumerians? Egyptology? Mesoamerica?

"I'm a creationist," Clifford Wilson said candidly. In case you don't know, creationists are Bible believers who reject the theory of evolution. According to their conviction, God literally created the Earth in six days and on the sixth day he also created man. For Creationists, there is no slow evolution from monkey to prehuman, and there was certainly no outside intervention. I learned that Dr. Clifford Wilson had written several books on the Bible and on Jesus.[6] This new knowledge of Wilson also made it obvious in which kitchen the anti-Däniken porridge had been cooked. Heaven help me!

In Germany, too, an anti-book was published shortly after I published *Chariots of the Gods*.[7] The author, Gerhard Gadow, was then studying law at a Berlin university. We met, and I learned that, once again, a professor of archeology (who doesn't want his name published) was behind the text. The then-youthful Gadow knew nothing of my publications before *Chariots of the Gods*. For this reason, I confess after decades of silence: at that time I invited anti-Däniken author Gerhard Gadow to the United States, and together we traveled around the United States for twenty days. Gerhard, a reliable companion, supervised the technology during my lectures. Later he wrote an excellent book on the Atlantis dispute.[8]

That's life! Up and down, praise and hostility go together. Thank God we don't live in a world where *par ordre du mufti* (decisions not based on facts) must be believed.

The American AAS was eventually joined by more and more intelligent and scientifically trained people. Some members defended my views and even published books on these subjects. Some examples are Hans Schindler Bellamy, archeologist and author of a book on Tiahuanaco; Luis E. Navia, a professor at the New York Institute of Technology; Dr. David Horn, anthropologist and professor at Colorado State University; and Josef F. Blumrich, one-time Chief Engineer of NASA.[9] They all wrote books that supported the hypothesis of a prehistoric visit from outer space. In addition, I received ideological support from Nobel-laureate Francis Crick and from Dr. Chandra Wickramasinghe, one of the most important astronomers and now director of the Buckingham Center for Astrobiology at the University of Buckingham (England).[10] The list of his publications is endless. After all, we had all learned in school that life on Earth was created in a primordial soup in which atoms finally formed into molecular chains. Dr. Wickramasinghe refuted this old idea in absolutely scientific fashion. "The theory of a primordial soup is utter nonsense," says the scholar today. "The origin of life came from outside the Earth."[11]

INSIDE SPACE COMMAND

In 1984, a member of the AAS and a senior US Air Force officer, who still does not want his name published, gave me access to Air Force Space Command. What's this? Near Colorado Springs, Colorado, in the middle of the Rocky Mountains, are some hollowed-out mountain ranges. These house Air Force Space Command, which is responsible for the total surveillance of outer space. I visited the site on August 2, 1984, and relearned the art of being amazed.

Today, Space Command (now headquartered at Peterson Air Force Base, Colorado) is three times more extensive than it was in 1984—if I visited now, my amazement would probably be endless. Fans of the TV series *Stargate* occasionally catch a glimpse of the entrance I used and do not even know that the facility actually exists. Cheyenne Mountain Complex is what is written on the cliff above the huge entrance gate. This gate is actually a safe door: it is 3 meters high, 4 meters wide, and weighs a good 25 tons. A few meters behind it, there is a second door of the same caliber. Behind that are several rock hangars of different sizes. The walls, ceilings, connecting galleries, and elevators are secured against falling rock with steel nets and heavy concrete. None of the subterranean spaces are in direct contact with the rock; they are all isolated in the massive domes. The space is also safe against nuclear attacks. Even if a rock wall trembled, the rooms would remain untouched because each also stands on steel springs that each weigh 500 kilograms. Inside, people sit in front of computers and on the walls are several large screens.

What I had to keep silent about decades ago, I can write about today. During my visit, a yellow alarm light suddenly lit up. The officer accompanying me pushed me into the next empty chair and placed his index finger over his lips. The room was silent except for the sound of everybody typing on keyboards. Not a word was spoken. Then, suddenly, projected onto a wall on the left, a fire appeared, seemingly from a volcanic eruption. Moments later, a zoom lens picked up on a rocket that slowly peeled out of a silo and picked up speed. Then I saw the outlines of parts of the Soviet Union, of Europe, and Alaska. Numbers and trajectories appeared on the large-scale projection on the right, and finally a crossed-out sign of radioactivity. What happened?

Even during the Cold War of the time, the United States and the Soviet Union informed each other about the launch of intercontinental missiles. This made it less likely that either country could accidentally trigger a nuclear war. However, on that August 2, 1984, the Soviets launched an underground rocket that had not been reported to the United States. Space Command satellites tracked the engine's thrusters before the projectile left the silo. The exact geographical location of the rocket was communicated to another satellite with incredible "viewing technology." A zoom lens filmed the rocket as soon as it came out of the silo. Computers calculated its size, speed, and trajectory, and another satellite measured whether any radioactivity was aboard the projectile. All of this technology was already in use in 1984.

What might monitoring technology look like today? About 1200 active satellites surround the Earth. The ISS (the International Space Station) orbits our planet every 91 minutes at an altitude of 400 kilometers. So do thousands of pieces of space junk. Space Command must have everything under control. No satellite is allowed to collide with the garbage. As early as

1984, the people at the computers could tell me exactly where the latest Soyuz spacecraft was moving. Not the projected position, but the real position above the earth. The system of sensors misses no missile launch. As soon as a satellite registers something out of the ordinary—whether it is a volcanic eruption or a bush fire—it reports the event directly to the early warning room. All unusual details are sent to the five projectors. Depending on the location of the fired rocket, it can take around 1600 seconds to reach the American continent. When the rockets are launched from a submarine, the flight time can be as little as 600 seconds.

The computers know immediately which sensors reported the event. That way you know the launch time, the exact position of the launching pad, the starting speed and the direction of the projectile, what type of missile is involved, and much more. The impact location can be determined to a vicinity of 100 meters. Space Command also knows the position of each submarine no matter which ocean it is moving in right now. Creepy.

Of course, when I was there, I also wanted to know if Space Command had targeted UFOs.

"Unknown echoes keep coming up." I remarked. "What are you doing about it?"

"Nothing. The things are so fast, perform impossible maneuvers, and disappear like a ghost. They cannot come from any earthly power and are therefore classified as irrelevant. No danger to national security. Our planes can't track them anyway. It all happens in outer space."

SECRET LECTURE AT NASA

My "relationship boxes," as they are popularly known, also include secret lectures and contacts that I should not yet talk about. But *temporas mutantur*, times are changing, and we change with them. In the fall of 1972, I held a lecture in Huntsville, Alabama. Why keep it secret? The invitation was organized by a high-ranking NASA employee, and both parties agreed to secrecy. Huntsville was once a boring little village on the edge of the Appalachian Mountains. Then came NASA, and the former cotton town turned into a technology park. Factories, laboratories, rocket test rigs, giant hangars, and administrative offices sprang up within a very short time. The Huntsville residents call their city Rocket City.

The crème de la crème of NASA met at my secret speech, including the rocket builders Dr. Pscherra, Dr. Slattery, Dr. Stuhlinger, Dr. Singer, Dr. Debus, and of course, the head of the construction department, Josef Blumrich. Initially Blumrich was very skeptical about my theories. But then he did a lot of studies on the so-called "visions" of the biblical prophet Ezekiel and admitted: "Seldom has a total defeat been so rewarding, so fascinating, and so delightful."[12]

INTERNATIONAL RELATIONS NETWORKS

A similar reversal of values occurred for Dr. Pasqual Schievella, President of the National Council for Critical Analysis in New York. Formerly an opponent of my hypotheses, he became a member of the AAS after examining all the sources, saying, "The AAS does not expect more from the world than to be allowed to pursue its ideas in the same spirit as science and that its findings are received with the same respectful attention as those of other sciences."

But so far everything I've told you takes place in America—what about my connections with Europeans and with Russians?

In Germany, I got to know the astronauts Dr. Ulf Merbold, Dr. Reinhard Furrer, and Dr. Ulrich Walter in person, the latter being the holder of the Chair of Space Technology (I also gave a lecture at his institute). Dr. Walter's predecessor Dr. Harry O. Ruppe and I have been friends for decades. Ruppe worked for a long time as Wernher von Braun's right-hand man at NASA in Huntsville and is the author of several books on space travel.

In the former Soviet Union, it was the cosmonaut Georgy Mikhailovich Grechko who sought contact with me and I was invited to give two (again) secret lectures in Moscow and St. Petersburg. In 1979, Grechko was the record holder for time spent in orbit. He had spent a total of 135 days in weightlessness. He is a twice-named hero of the Soviet Union and a statue was erected in his honor in a park near St. Petersburg. We visited the statue together on a cold winter night.

Like the US astronaut and moon traveler Edgar Mitchell, Grechko stayed with me in Beatenberg,

Switzerland. Both astronauts visited the Mystery Park in Interlaken, a fabulous theme park that deals with the great mysteries of the world (it has since been renamed Jungfrau Park). There, visitors are offered an attraction called Sputnik. It is a capsule that stands on hydraulic stilts, which move quickly and can shake up the visitors while they are in it. Passengers of the capsule are buckled in, and in front of their eyes is a three-dimensional screen. It creates the illusion of a space flight on re-entry into the earth's atmosphere. Grechko, then record holder in outer space, stood outside in front of the capsule and followed its abrupt movements. An employee of the park, not knowing who he was asked Grechko:

FIGURE 5.1: *Apollo 14 Astronaut Dr. Edgar Mitchell*

"Would you like to take a ride? It's like the illusion of a spaceflight."

"Spaceflight?" Grechko replied, rolling his eyes in front of the youthful employee. "Spaceflight? Never in my life would I risk such a thing!"

CHAPTER 6

What I Also
Wanted to Say . . .

For thousands of years, people have written about aliens. However, our ancestors did not call them *aliens* but *gods*. Their deeds, their weapons, their vehicles, and their behavior were described in these writings.[1]

Actually Earth would have likely drowned in hymns and praises in honor of these heavenly beings. Thousands of years ago events were global, affecting all people. But where are the hundreds of thousands of written testimonies about alien visits?

They are everywhere, and they can also be found in the sacred books of ancient religions. But clever beings as we are, we have hidden them from ourselves by translating all these stories only in a religious-psychological way. Because we are ignorant of other lifeforms in the universe, spaceship commanders became *gods*, astronauts became *angels*, a shuttle flight became an *ascension*, and a stay on the mother spaceship became a visit to *heaven.* Holy simplicity! But yes—that is *what I also wanted to say*—in our culture of debates we forget the most important thing:

Once Pharaoh Ramses III (1221–1156 BC) assembled a huge library. Nothing is left of it. When Caesar allowed his troops to ravage the port of Alexandria in 48 BC, the library also went up in flames. Seven hundred thousand volumes gone. Cleopatra was given 200,000 volumes from the Library of Pergamum of Ancient Greece in 43 BC. They formed the foundation of the new library of Alexandria. But again, the Roman emperor Diocletian (244–313 AD) destroyed everything. Even the third attempt to bring the Alexandrian library to glory and wealth by collecting ancient writings failed. Theodosius I (347–395 AD), to whom the nickname "the Great" was erroneously attached, had the library burned down again. And in the year 562 of our era, the Caliph of Damascus, Umar ibn al-Chattab (579–644 AD) burned the books of the Mouseion at Alexandria to heat all the baths of the city for six months until no more writings were available.

In his campaigns, Julius Caesar had libraries destroyed; Alexander the Great did the same with the writings of Awesta. These were the original religious texts of the Parses.

In China, it was Emperor Qin Shihuangdi (259–210 BC) who had all the libraries of his defeated enemies burned down.

The same happened in Ethiopia. Italian soldiers fired up the old royal libraries of Addis Ababa. Valuable writings ended up in the Vatican Library in Rome, where they are still untranslated today. It was the same in South and Central America. On June 12, 1562, Bishop Diego de Landa (1524–1579 AD) burned all Mayan manuscripts in public. For him, the old gods who had once come down from heaven were just superstitious, stupid ideas.

The vast library of Nalanda University (now Bihar State, India) was completely destroyed by Turkish conqueror Bakhtiyar Khilji (died 1206). Because of the huge number of books, the fire burned for over three months.

Christian rulers weren't any better. In 1242, instigated by Pope Gregory IX (1227–1241), in the so-called "Talmud-burning" in Paris, twenty-four truckloads of Jewish books were torched. The writings had been collected from the whole kingdom of France. For two days the piles burned.

Orders for book burnings were also issued by Popes Innocent IV (1243–1254), Clement IV (1256–1268), John XXII (1316–1334), Paul IV (1555–1559), and others into modern times.

In 1559, the *Index Librorum Prohibitorum* appeared—the directory of forbidden books. Any Catholic who read a work from this prohibited list was automatically excommunicated—excluded from the church and its sacraments. The last official issue of the *Index Librorum Prohibitorum* appeared in May 1948.

The reasons for the destruction of billions of books were always the same: arrogance and a know-it-all attitude. Neither the secular nor the religious leaders could admit that older and much larger cultures existed before their own, that there had once been other religions initiated by someone from somewhere else in the universe. Thousands of years ago, people "ascended to heaven," and not just the savior of their new religion, whether it was Jesus, Buddha, or XY.

If we were in possession of the old books, there would not be a need for a guy like me. My colleagues and I would not have to laboriously search for clues in old texts. It would be common knowledge: once aliens landed on Earth. Our Stone Age ancestors understood nothing and mistakenly believed that these extraterrestrials were gods. The so-called gods in turn behaved like ethnologists. They studied some tribes, learned a few languages, gave some advice, and then disappeared "into heaven." However, they promised to return in the distant future. Everything would be crystal clear *if the old books had not been destroyed.*

Has humanity learned anything from it?

The destruction of scriptures and other cultural assets continues unabashedly in our time. Hitler had books burned publicly, and every idiotic dictator gets rid of disagreeable magazines and newspapers, arresting or killing the authors. Today, in the name of religions, not only libraries but also sanctuaries and statues of the hated cultures are razed to the ground. That's how far civilization has gone. It is just watching and not interfering. It is doing nothing, appearing powerless.

This powerlessness regarding the destroyed, distorted, matted, and religiously distorted texts is joined by ineradicable human stubbornness. I experience it worldwide and every day. Whether it's grandiose structures in Central or South America, Egypt, or Asia, the response is the same everywhere. What? The construction of our sanctuaries was influenced from outside our Earth? You dare to downgrade the achievements of our ancestors? By this way of national thinking, all objectivity is brushed aside. The actual mission for archeology is no longer the acquisition of knowledge, but of national pride. A direct line is drawn from the millennia-old building structures to our own past. We are the greatest! Our ancestors were the greatest! And everything that speaks against this is angrily rejected.

Some ancient Arab historians wrote that the Great Pyramid was built by Saurid, a ruler before the Flood, and that Saurid was the same person the Hebrews called Enoch. I believe that such historical transition can only be nonsense. Such statement would have to assume that Jews participated in the construction of the pyramids. Impossible! According to this logic, gods could never have been visitors from other solar systems. Then we would not be the greatest anymore. And because tour guides and national archaeologists simply won't accept it, of course it was *people* who built the grand temples and pyramids. Of course people created the phenomenal works of art. The gods never got their hands dirty. (With the exception of a few small base camps that they erected.) All of the architectural and master craft pieces are human works. But the original impulse that answered the question "*Why* did people do it?" came from outside. This can be proved, even if it does not fit the national pride. The musicians of the Berlin Symphony Orchestra don't feel humiliated when they play *Rhapsody in Blue* just because the composer George Gershwin was an American.

The past is falsified in situ, books were and are being destroyed. And although all modern states promise free opinion and the free word in their constitutions and basic laws, neither politicians nor courts adhere to this. In Article 5, the German Basic Law guarantees that "Everyone has the right to freely express and disseminate his opinion in written, spoken and illustrated terms. Freedom of the press and freedom of reporting are guaranteed. Censorship does not take place."

Quite similar are statements in the Swiss Federal Constitution; for instance, if you read Article 16 paragraph 2: "Each person has the right to form their opinion freely and to freely express and disseminate it." In 1946, the UN declared freedom of information as a fundamental human right. In the US, the Freedom of Information Act guarantees freely accessible information. What has become of it?

Through our media channels, society is fed uniform news. Every day, manipulation is trickling in. People become dumb moralists who pretend to be "good people." Their world view is being prepared in secret offices, and the editors and chiefs at the front are merely henchmen of superfluous councils, advisory councils, political commissions, and calculators of quotas, who interfere at every inappropriate opportunity, although they do not understand anything at all. This is demonstrated perfectly when it comes to genetic engineering or the nuclear accident of Fukushima, Japan. As is known, that accident led to the energy turnaround. (No more nuclear power in German-speaking Europe!) A fairytale that is incompatible with reality is spread in all leading media about this accident. (19,000 died from radiation poisoning! Ha!). And everyone who knows the truth is condemned to silence because the media does not pass on any other information.

All our brains are gelatinized. There is moral cowardice. Moral courage? Forget it! And whoever stands up against it is drowned in the swamp of egalitarianism. Programs with views that contradict the great religions must not exist ("This has nothing to do with Islam . . . "). The public discussion about carbon dioxide is no different. That CO_2 has hardly anything to do with the climate change is also known to thousands of scientists. But they are never allowed to speak. The advisory councils, or better, the lobbyists, know how to prevent that. A free society? The free word is constitutionally guaranteed? Hilarious! The aliens are probably calling the third planet in this solar system the Planet of Lies. That's where we are today. Ignorance and the belief in some humbug clearly dominate.

Young people fidget around on their smart phones, screens spit data into their retinas, which they are not actually interested in, and therefore it disappears again into the chamber of oblivion.

Even though we surf the Internet for information, we do not dive into it. The Internet manipulates us because we believe that we can retrieve all information on the web and be fully informed. But behind every piece of information are people with opinions—even religious and political ones. Someone has, somewhere and at some time, typed or scanned an opinion into the network. Thus, not only do lightning-fast truths race around the earth, but untruths do as well. And the cunning intelligence agencies that register x billions of electronic information are also saving x billions of lies. A fabulous system!

Being able to get true information over the Internet is an illusion. We are especially left in the dark when it comes to getting hold of ancient texts. Either they were never entered or they exist only in shortened or religiously sealed versions. (Giga garbage in, Giga garbage out). The omniscient Internet is already manipulating those of us who think we can count on it. Information is input by like-minded people for like-minded people. The daily Internet surfers, and I know wonderful types of them, all behave as if they're the same as soon as they sit in front of a keyboard. Just as if unconscious people were twitching to the same beat.

And in our fabulous world of constitutionally guaranteed information rights, politicians and judges just do not care. Those who should stand up for the rights, shrug their shoulders. Books and articles are banned by court orders because an individual, or even worse, a political ideology or religion, feels hurt. Texts are prevented by political correctness or gender smugness. The authors are dragged to court. Today, it's hard to believe, laws exist that scream for thought police. Who said that? Racist! The politically controlled mass consciousness, the Orwell state, has been realized. And the sad judges, who also enforce this nonsense of ideas, think that their judgments serve the peace of mind of society, which they think is more important than the constitution. When will there be supreme justices who will enforce the clear text and instill in our political clowns the truth that the constitution is above any law?

In other words, any law that prevents freedom of expression is unconstitutional? There are no exceptions in the respective constitutions, no "if it's . . ." or "except for . . . ." The human know-it-all attitude and stubbornness have always trampled over dead bodies and broken every law for thousands of years and, later, every constitution.

Oh yes, in our time, we hear of "bought journalists."[2] So their word only tells half of the story. I know excellent and brilliant journalists, none of whom are "bought." But they are all subject to the current zeitgeist, which does not allow them to write about certain hypotheses without prejudice or to talk about it in the editorial office. Colleagues could possibly get the wrong idea. Bought media? No. The truth is: they are concealing media.

NOTES

CHAPTER 1: IMPOSSIBLE ENCOUNTERS

1. L. Pauwels and J. Bergier, *Aufbruch ins dritte Jahrtausend* (Bern, 1962).

2. *Der Spiegel* No. 31 (1991).

3. n-tv (Deutschland): *Die Wahrheit über UFOs*, June 9, 2015.

4. Ronald Story, *The Encyclopedia of UFOs* (New York, 1980).

5. J. Allen Hynek, *The UFO Experience: A Scientific Inquiry* (Chicago, 1972); John G. Fuller, *The Interrupted Journey* (New York, 1974); John G. Fuller, *Aliens in the Skies* (New York, 1969); Johannes von Buttlar, *Das UFO-Phänomen* (Munich, 1978); Erich von Däniken, *Der Götterschock* (Munich, 1992), S. 195 ff.

6. "The Zeta Reticuli Incident," *Astronomy*, December 1974; Terence Dickinson, *The Zeta Reticuli Incident* (Milwaukee, reprint, 1976); Wilhelm Gliese, *Catalog of Nearby Stars* (San Francisco, 1969).

7. Dr. Allen Hynek, *Bild am Sonntag*, June 6, 1976.

8. B. Hopkins, *Eindringlinge* (Hamburg, 1991).

9. W. Strieber, *Communion* (New York, 1987); Whitley Striebe *Transformation: The Breakthrough* (New York, 1988).

10. J. Fiebag, *Kontakt: UFO-Entführungen in Deutschland, Österreich und der Schweiz* (Munich, 1994).

11. John E. Mack, *Abduction: Human Encounters with Aliens* (New York, 1994).

12. Illobrand von Ludwiger, *Ergebnisse aus 40 Jahren UFO-Forschung* (Rottenburg, 2015), 222.

13. Leslie Kean, *UFOs: Generäle, Piloten und Regierungsvertreter brechen ihr Schweigen* (Rottenburg, 2010).

CHAPTER 2: FAIRYTALES FOR CHRISTIANS

1. Dr. F. M. Hassnain, correspondence with the author EvD-Archiv, No. 1584.

2. Erich von Däniken, *Reise nach Kiribati* (Düsseldorf, 1981).

3. Erich von Däniken, *Erscheinungen* (Düsseldorf, 1974), S. 128 ff.

4. von Däniken, *Reise*; von Däniken, *Erscheinungen*; Erich von Däniken, *Auf den Spuren der All-Mächtigen* (Munich, 1993).

5. Andreas Faber-Kaiser, *Jesus lebte und starb in Kaschmir* (Berlin, 1976; new edition, Berlin: Ullstein, 1998).

6. Johannes Lehmann, *Jesus-Report* (Düsseldorf, 1970).

7. Robert Kehl, *Die Religion des modernen Menschen*, Heft 6a. Zürich o. J.

8. Friedrich Delitzsch, *Die große Täuschung* (Stuttgart/ Berlin, 1921).

9. Dr. Dileep Kumar Kanjilal, correspondence with the author, EvD-Archiv, No. 1500.

10. Erich von Däniken, *Habe ich mich geirrt?* (Munich, 1985), S. 225 ff.

11. *Rigveda*,1.25.6,1.111.1, 1.20.3, 1.25.111.

12. *Rigveda*, 1.30.18–20.

13. Albert Ludwig, *Abhandlungen über das Ramayana und die Bezie-hungen desselben zum Mahabharata* (Prague, 1894).

14. Hermann Jacobi, *Das Ramayana* (Bonn, 1893).

15. Dileep Kumar Kanjilal, *Vimana in Ancient India* (Calcutta, 1991).

CHAPTER 3: EGYPTIAN CONNECTIONS

1. Erich von Däniken, *Die Augen der Sphinx* (Munich, 1989). S. 15 ff.

2. Adolf Wahrmund, *Diodor's von Sizilien Geschichtsbibliothek,* Erstes Buch (Stuttgart, 1866).

3. Raymond Oliver Faulkner, *The Ancient Egyptian Pyramid Texts* (Oxford, 1969); Kurt Sethe, *Übersetzung und Kommentar zu den altägyptischen Pyramidentexten,* Band II (Darmstadt, 1922).

4. "Portcullis Blocks Robot in Pyramid," *The Daily Telegraph,* London, April 7, 1993.

5. Telex Reuters and SDA from April 16, 1993.

6. *Mail on Saturday,* April 17, 1993.

7. "Secret Chamber May Solve Pyramid Riddle," *The Times,* April 17, 1993; Erich von Däniken, *Der Jüngste Tag hat längst begonnen* (Munich, 1995), S. 255 ff.

8. Erich von Däniken, *Der Mittelmeerraum und seine mysteriöse Vorzeit* (Rottenburg, 2012), S. 168 ff.

9. *National Geographic Society: Inside the Great Pyramid* (Nemesis, 2003).

10. Luc Bürgin, *Mysteries,* No. 21(Basel, April 2011).

CHAPTER 4: LIED TO, CHEATED, ABUSED

1. Ferdinand Schmid, Karl Brugger, and FUNAI, correspondence with the author, EvD-Archiv, No. 1669.

2. Karl Brugger, *Die Chronik von Akakor* (Düsseldorf, 1976).

3. Brugger, *Chronik von Akakor*.

4. Wolfgang Siebenhaar, *Die Wahrheit über die Chronik von Akakor* (Rottenburg, 2006).

5. Friedrich Schleiermacher, *Platons Werke: Dritter Theil, erster Band—Der Staat* (Berlin, 1828).

6. Siebenhaar, *Die Wahrheit*.

7. Felicitas Barreto, correspondence with the author, EvD-Archiv, No. 467.

8. "Ich bin Tatunca. Punkt." *Der Spiegel*, No. 27 (2014).

9. Erich von Däniken, *Falsch informiert!* (Rottenburg: 2007).

10. Stan Hall, *Tayos Gold: The Archives of Atlantis* (Quito 2005); Stan Hall, *Tayos Fever* (London: 2007).

11. Alex Chionetti, http://www.Goldlibrary.com.

12. *Kebra Nagast, Die Herrlichkeit der Könige*, First edition (Munich: 1905).

13. "Ich habe die Bundeslade gesehen," *Mysteries*, No. 5 (Basel: September/October 2009).

14. Abarzua/Posselt, "Gräber aus uralter Zeit: Tote von anderen Sternen" *Bild*, 29 (April 1975).

15. Erich von Däniken, *Reise nach Kiribati* (Düsseldorf, 1982).

16. Erich von Däniken, *Grüße aus der Steinzeit* (Rottenburg, 2010), 170.

17. "Indio-Kultur im Dschungel," *Der Spiegel*, February 1, 1981.

18. Erich von Däniken, *Unmögliche Wahrheiten* (Rottenburg, 2013), 157.

19. Erich von Däniken, *Meine Welt in Bildern* (Düsseldorf, 1973).

20. Dr. Heather Lechtman, Article in *Spektrum der Wissenschaft*, August 1984.

21. Dr. Gebhardt, letter to Erich von Däniken, November 29, 1972, EvD-Archiv.

22. Peter Kaufhold, *Von den Göttern verlassen* (Recklinghausen, 1983).

23. Charles Berlitz, *Geheimnisse versunkener Welten* (Frankfurt, 1973).

24. Däniken, *Falsch informiert!*

CHAPTER 5: HIDDEN CONNECTIONS

1. Clifford Wilson, *Crash Go the Chariots* (New York, 1972).

2. Erich von Däniken, *Zeichen für die Ewigkeit* (München, 1997); Erich von Däniken, *Unmögliche Wahrheiten* (Rottenburg, 2013) p. 196 ff.

3. David and George Stuart, *Palenque: Eternal City of the Maya* (London, 2008).

4. Josef Blumrich, *Da tat sich der Himmel auf. Die Raumschiffe des Propheten Hesekiel* (Düsseldorf, 1973); Hans Herbert Beier, *Kronzeuge Ezechiel. Sein Bericht—sein Tempel—seine Raumschiffe* (Munich, 1985).

5. Erich von Däniken, "Erhielten unsere Vorfahren Besuch aus dem Weltall?" *The Northwest*, Winnipeg, Canada, December 8, 1964.

6. Clifford Wilson, *Exploring the Old Testament* (Word of Truth Productions, 1970); Clifford Wilson, *Jesus the Teacher* (Baker House, 1975); Clifford Wilson, *That Incredible Book, The Bible* (Pyramid Publications, 1975).

7. Gerhard Gadow, *Erinnerungen an die Wirklichkeit* (Frankfurt, 1971)

8. Gerhard Gadow, *Der Atlantis-Streit* (Frankfurt, 1972).

9. H. S. Bellamy, *The Great Idol of Tiahuanaco* (Faber and Faber, 1959); Luis E. Navia, *Unsere Wiege steht im Kosmos* (Düsseldorf, 1976); David A. Horn, *Der außerirdische Ursprung der Menschheit* (1997); J. F. Blumrich, *Kaskara und die sieben Welten* (Düsseldorf, 1979).

10. Francis Crick, *Life Itself* (New York, 1981).

11. Chandra Wickramasinghe, lecture on April 11, 2015, in the Festhalle Sindelfingen.

12. Josef E. Blumrich, *The Spaceships of Ezechiel* (London 1974); Harry O. Ruppe, *Die grenzenlose Dimension Raumfahrt* (Düsseldorf, 1980).

CHAPTER 6: WHAT I ALSO WANTED TO SAY...

1. The ten sources I mention here are the tip of the iceberg: Dileep Kumar Kanjilal, *Vimana in Ancient India* (Calcutta: 1991); Armin Risi, *Gott und die Götter* (Zürich: 1995); Willi Grömling, *Tibets altes Geheimnis: Gesar, ein Sohn des Himmels* (Groß-Gerau: 2005); Hermann Burgard, *Encheduana. Verschlüsselt, verschollen, verkannt* (Groß-Gerau: 2014); Potrap Chandra Roy, *The Mahabharata* (Calcutta: 1896); Nath M. Dutt, *The Ramayana* (Calcutta 1891); Protap Chandra Roy, *The Mahabharata, Vol. VI: Drona Parva* (Calcutta 1893); Emil Kautsch, *Die Apokryphen und Pseudepigraphen des Alten Testamentes, Band II: Das Buch Henoch* (Tübingen: 1900); Carl Bezold, *Kebra Nagast: Die Herrlichkeit der Könige. 23. Band,* First Edition (Munich, 1905); Paul Riessler, *Altjüdisches Schrifttum außerhalb der Bibel. Die Apokalypse des Abraham* (Augsburg: 1928).

2. Udo Ulfkotte, *Gekaufte Journalisten* (Rottenburg: 2014).

ABOUT THE AUTHOR

Erich von Däniken is arguably the most widely read and most copied nonfiction author in the world. He published his first (and best-known) book, *Chariots of the Gods*, in 1968. The worldwide bestseller was followed by forty more books, including the recent bestsellers *The Gods Never Left Us*, *Twilight of the Gods*, *History Is Wrong*, *Evidence of the Gods*, *Remnants of the Gods*, and *Odyssey of the Gods*. His works have been translated into twenty-eight languages and have sold more than sixty-five million copies. Several have also been made into films. Von Däniken's ideas have been the inspiration for a wide range of television series, including the History Channel's hit *Ancient Aliens*. His research organization, the AAS-RA/legendarytimes. com (Archaeology, Astronauts and SETI Research Association), comprises laymen and academics from all walks of life. Internationally, there are about 10,000 members. Erich lives in Switzerland but is an ever-present figure on the international lecture circuit, traveling more than 100,000 miles a year.

A NOTE FROM ERICH

As in each of my books, I would like to introduce you to the Archeology, Astronauts, and SETI Research Association (AAS-RA). We are looking for new answers, because the old ones are outdated in many areas.

It is our goal to provide recognized proof of alien visits to Earth that happened thousands of years ago. In doing so, we want to follow the basic rules of gaining scientific knowledge, but we do not want to be limited by existing dogmas or paradigms.

Every two months, we publish the magazine *Sagenhafte Zeiten* (*Legendary Times*), which is distributed to all members of the AAS. We organize national and international conferences and organize trips to interesting archaeological sites.

Our annual membership fee is 49 Euro /57 Swiss Francs (as of autumn 2013). Scientists and laypeople from all professions are welcome to join us. We are not an exclusive club.

I would be glad if you request free information from:

AAS, Postfach, CH-3803 Beatenberg Switzerland
www.sagenhaftezeiten.com
info@sagenhaftezeiten.com